ALSO BY PETER OSBORNE

The Port Jervis Area Heritage Commission Salutes the Gilded Age

*The Port Jervis Area Heritage Commission Salutes
the Old Decker Stone House*

*The New York-New Jersey Boundary Dispute:
While New Jersey Dozed, New York was Wide Awake*

Graveyard Art and its History

The Chartering of the City of Port Jervis: 1907-1997

*We Can Take It: The Roosevelt Tree Army at New Jersey's High Point State
Park 1933-1941*

*Images of America: High Point State Park and the Civilian Conservation
Corps*
Images of America: Hacklebarney and Voorhees State Parks

Images of America: Promised Land State Park

The Delaware River Heritage Trail Guide

*Our Town: Historic Port Jervis 1907-2007
Co-authored with Daniel Dwyer*

VIGILANCE  PERSEVERANCE

Courtesy Brian Lewis

Fort Decker, 2004

VIGILANCE & PERSEVERANCE

THE HISTORY OF THE OLD DECKER STONE HOUSE

BY
PETER OSBORNE

Minisink Press

Port Jervis, New York

Published by Minisink Press
An imprint of Minisink Valley Historical Society
127-131 West Main Street
Post Office Box 659
Port Jervis, New York 12771

First Edition, published 2007
10 9 8 7 6 5 4 3 2 1

ISBN 978-0978739928

Library of Congress Control Number: 2007900457

Cover design by Rick Hibberd

Book designed by Peter Osborne

Manuscript read and edited by Robert Aber, Flojean Collette, Nancy Conod, Mark Hendrickson, Janis Osborne, Charles Swartwout, Nancy Vocci, Barbara and Fred Johnson Weissman.

Printed in the United States of America

Preserving the Minisink Valley region's history
for more than one hundred years.

Visit us on the Internet at www.minisink.org

Courtesy Minisink Valley Historical Society

Dedicated to the memory
of
Richard G. Tarbell

Richard Tarbell (1950-2002) served on the board of directors of the Minisink Valley Historical Society for more than twenty years. He was a faithful and loyal servant of the organization and had a great interest in seeing Fort Decker preserved. Richard was also instrumental in creating the public programming at the Fort.

TABLE OF CONTENTS

Native Americans had been living in the region for more than 12,000 years. Within two generations of the arrival of Europeans they were largely dispersed or gone from the area.

The Old Mine Road is said to be the first one-hundred-mile road in America built by early Dutch explorers in the mid-1600s. While the theory remains controversial, there is no doubt that the road led European settlers into the Delaware Valley in the early eighteenth century.

Tradition has it that the Hayne family occupied the building now called Fort Decker. Very little, however, is known about them.

While no images exist, it is believed that the trading post built on the current site was a blockhouse that may even be contained within the foundation of the present-day building.

Jervis. It included the flats along the Delaware River and may have extended to and along the Neversink River.

THE ST. JOHN HOTEL - PAGE 113

Another important moment in the building's history occurred when it was a hotel used by Delaware and Hudson Canal engineers in the first quarter of the nineteenth century.

THE DECKER STONE HOUSE IN THE NINETEENTH CENTURY - PAGE 125

While much of the nineteenth century history of the building is shrouded in mystery, the John Cannon Sr. family that owned it after 1872 was determined to own it for one hundred years.

THE DECKER STONE HOUSE IN THE TWENTIETH CENTURY - PAGE 137

As any long-time resident of Port Jervis will know, the family most associated with the building in recent living memory is the Campfield family who lived in the building for almost sixty years.

FORT DECKER AS A MUSEUM - PAGE 149

Through the efforts of many dedicated people the Decker Stone House is now a museum. It could easily have been demolished leaving only a historic marker.

WHO TURNS ON THE LIGHTS AT 9:15? - PAGE 167

Visitors to Fort Decker and students of the building's history always ask - "Is the building haunted?" There are five potential spiritual visitors who may turn on the lights.

INTRODUCTION

On the corner of West Main and Old West Main Streets in the City of Port Jervis, New York, stands a stone building that has witnessed many dramatic moments in our community's history. The "Old Stone House," as it was known in the nineteenth century, witnessed the transformation of forested river bottom land to an isolated wilderness settlement, then into a small city that remains at the crossroads of the region's major transportation arteries. It is probably the oldest building within the City's limits.

The stone house has been the scene of significant historical events and activities. First, in the mid-eighteenth century it served as a trading post run by Frederick Hayne; during the American Revolution it served as a frontier military fort owned by Lt. Martinus Decker, and finally, during the early years of the nineteenth century, as a hotel for the Delaware and Hudson Canal Company's engineers. After which it became a private residence until the 1950s. Since 1970, it has been owned and operated by the Minisink Valley Historical Society (MVHS), Orange County's second oldest historical organization. The structure, with its simple but beautiful lines, is one of the city's most important landmarks.

For the last twenty-six years I have been collecting information with the intention of someday writing a definitive history on Martinus Decker and his stone house. In 1993 I completed a booklet on the history of the stone house to commemorate the 200th anniversary of its rebuilding. For the first time since the Society purchased it, all of the known data about the building was compiled and placed in a format for visitors to read. This new effort brings forth new information that has been uncovered since then, including interviews with people who had some part in the house's recent history, the gleaning of data from various sources in the MVHS archives, and observations that I have made about the building in my time here.

Incorporated in the telling of this story are the results of the archaeological work done in 1982, 1998 and 1999 by the Society and the Orange County Chapter of the New York State Archaeological Association. Test pits were dug in the basement of the building and around the foundation's exterior. As a result we began to undertake some long-needed projects, including the creation of an archive of materials about the building's history.

Another important addition to this body of research was locating and transcribing Lt. Martinus Decker's Revolutionary War service records. Many of those records, including the genealogy page from the family's Bible, have never been published, and have only been seen by a handful of researchers since the 1830s. I believe the bibliography included at the end is the most comprehensive ever compiled about the building, and will assist future researchers as they try to shed more light on the lives of the people who lived in the stone house.

The most colorful person associated with the house was Martinus Decker. One cannot help but be impressed by him even though relatively little is known about him. One can only imagine what his Revolutionary War military service entailed, or what his life was like, from the distance of two hundred years. Decker's personal motto was "Vigilance and Perseverance." He was held in high regard by his contemporaries as evidenced by legal affidavits that were filed long after his death. During the American Revolution he was at Fort Montgomery on the Hudson River just before and after it was destroyed by the British in 1777. He was responsible for the capture of two spies north of Port Jervis, and helped guard the mountain passes in the Sloatsburg, New York area. Martinus Decker's home was used as a fort, and burned during Joseph Brant's raid into the Minisink region in 1779.

He rebuilt his house in 1793 at the age of sixty, and he lived to see the dawn of a new century. The decades that followed would see his family's farm partitioned and sold to the Delaware and Hudson Canal Company, and to the Erie Railroad for its Delaware Division yards and shops. All were constructed on what had been his pastures and fields.

It is an honor to have been Fort Decker's caretaker for the last twenty-six years; as each year passes, I am more humbled by that position, and have an even greater respect for the builder's skills. I often think about the people who have lived there, because over the last two hundred and fifty years there have been births and deaths in the building, along with weddings, happy and sad moments. If the walls could talk, I am sure they could tell many stories.

My favorite time of the year in the building is early spring, when I stand on the front porch and imagine the houses directly in front are not yet built, and I can see the farm fields, the wonderful view the Deckers had when they came out of their house in the morning. The Delaware River is to the west, Mt. William to the north, the river-bottom lands that were so productive for the Anglo-Dutch farmers to the east, and then, the Shawangunk Ridge to the southeast.

Having worked on a number of old buildings during my career, I have come to the conclusion that they have spirits, and look kindly upon the people and organizations who care for them. I believe the Decker Stone House stands a little taller because of the many people who have maintained and preserved it since its construction. As we remember almost two hundred and fifty years of history at the stone house, we rededicate our efforts for the generations yet to come.

Peter Osborne
Executive Director
Minisink Valley Historical Society
July 22, 2007

The Original People

Native Americans had been living in the Minisink region for about 12,000 years prior to the first European settlers coming to the Delaware Valley in the 1690s. The oldest human occupation site east of the Mississippi River is just twenty-five miles east of Port Jervis at the Dutchess Quarry cave site in Florida, New York. *(For purposes of simplification and for the reader's ease, Port Jervis is used as a geographical reference point in this manuscript even though the city did not get its name until 1827.)* It is believed that Paleo Indians, the earliest indigenous people in America, occupied that site. The Paleo Indians were a hunting culture, and their main quarry was the mastodon. Some have suggested they may have hunted this large elephant-like animal into extinction.

The next group of people to live in the valley were called the Archaic, and they were hunters and gatherers. They lived in the region from 8,000 B.C.E. to 1,000 B.C.E. There have been many Archaic sites found in the Upper Delaware region north of Port Jervis. The last group of native people who were active in the area were the Woodland group or the Lenapes. They lived here from about 1,000 B.C.E. until about 1745 when they began

Courtesy Minisink Valley Historical Society

The Minisink Region.

to move westward. They are the Indians most people are familiar with; they were hunters and gatherers who generally stayed at
a communal site for about eight years. There are several known
Woodland sites in the Delaware valley south of Port Jervis, and
along the Neversink and Delaware Rivers including the area
where Fort Decker is located.

There is at least one description of what the flatlands
looked like along both the Delaware and Neversink Rivers. Peter
Gumaer, author of the **History of Deerpark,** wrote "The flats
were covered with a tall grass from four to six feet high, and the
same and surrounding, often burned over, abounded with deer,
bears, raccoons and many smaller animals suitable for the suste-

Courtesy Minisink Valley Historical Society

This mortar and pestle were used to grind corn and grains. Corn was a mainstay of the Lenape diet.

nance of man . . . The rivers teemed with different kinds of fishes."

Archaeological work completed at Fort Decker has turned up a corner of one Woodland Era point, about four feet below the surface of the soil in the area now occupied by the herb garden. It may have been broken as it was being worked on by the maker. Lenape people used items like pecking stones, scrapers, axes and projectile points that are still occasionally found in farm fields.

The relationship between the native people and early settlers, at least until the early years of the French and Indian War (1758-1763), seems to have been a relatively peaceful one. Fort Decker served in its early years as a trading post between the Native Americans and settlers. One of the most important components of that relationship was the fur trade which supplied furs for a growing domestic market in England, and in return provided the Lenape with finished goods.

In a story that was

Courtesy Minisink Valley Historical Society

This broken arrow point was found in the area now occupied by the Society's herb garden in 1982.

Courtesy Peter Osborne

The river flatlands where Fort Decker was built was probably covered by tall grasses that stretched for miles.

repeated throughout the eighteenth and nineteenth centuries, Native Americans were either forced off their ancestral lands as increasing numbers of settlers pushed west, or their lands were purchased, and they moved westward into Pennsylvania and Ohio. By 1745, after having inhabited this area for about 12,000 years, most of the native people were either gone or had been assimilated into the general population. The only group left was a small tribe that lived near present-day Cahoonzie.

There are some archaeologists and historians that have uncovered what they say is information that would suggest the Iberians, Celts, Phoenicians or Romans were here long before the earliest European settlers. Calendar sites, perched boulders and stone piles dot the area, and it is known that the native peoples were not a lithic *(users of stone)* people. While this theory remains controversial, it would dramatically alter the history of the region if it is true.

The earliest known European settler to come into the southern Neversink River valley was William Tietsoort (Titsworth), who arrived in the 1690s. He was a blacksmith who carried on an active trade with the local Native Americans. Soon,

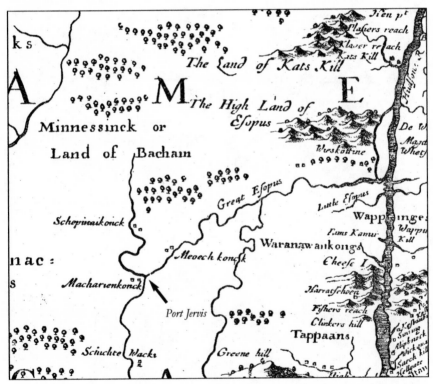

Courtesy Minisink Valley Historical Society

The Visscher map, as it is called, shows the approximate location of present-day Port Jervis, as indicated by the arrow at the junction of the Delaware and Neversink Rivers in the late 1600s.

a steady stream of Anglo-Dutch and French Huguenots, who were fleeing religious persecution in Europe, came into the area by proceeding southward along the Old Mine Road from Kingston, New York. The region was then known as "The Minisink" or "The Minisinks," as George Washington later referred to it in correspondence during the American Revolution. The Minisink Valley was known for its rich and abundant river-bottom land and fur trade.

THE OLD MINE ROAD: EARLY SETTLEMENT

Much controversy surrounds the history of the Old Mine Road, but it has been proposed that it is the first 100-mile-long road in America. Tradition has it that the road was built by Dutch explorers prior to 1664 to create an avenue for extracted copper ore to be shipped from crude mines in Pahaquarry, New Jersey, just a short distance north of the Delaware Water Gap. While most historians have focused on the copper connection, the entire Shawangunk Ridge *(as it is called in New York)* and the Kittaninny Ridge *(as it is called in New Jersey)* contained various minerals, a potential source of income for the Dutch explorers prior to 1664. So the name "Old Mine Road" may actually reflect a broader context.

Critics of the Old Mine Road's history believe the road is not as old as claimed, and that the mining of copper ore in the large amounts suggested was physically impossible. Others contend that much of the Old Mine Road was a series of Indian trails widened by increased use. There is no argument, however, that the road was in existence after 1700. Present-day New York State Route 209 and New Jersey Sussex County Route 521 tra-

Courtesy Minisink Valley Historical Society

The Old Mine Road

verse the approximate route of the old road. In addition, the settlement of the region was made easier because of the existence of the road, which essentially bypassed the Shawangunk Mountains. For travelers, it made a much more circuitous route into the interior from New York and Kingston.

The road allowed the creation of two distinct settlements in the Neversink Valley. The first was at Peenpack, or the "Upper Neighborhood" as it was called; today the area is known as Godeffroy, New York. This settlement was carved out of the wilderness in the late 1690s and early 1700s by a group of French Huguenots including the Caudebec, Provost, Gumaer, Van Inwegen and Swartwout families. A second and distinct settlement, known as the "Lower Neighborhood," took in much of present-day Port Jervis. It was centered in the area where Jersey Avenue and East Main Streets meet, and spread out from there. The families that originally settled here, sometime after 1715, were the Deckers, Westfalls, Westbrooks, Coles, Davises, Caskeys and Cuykendalls, along with others. Many of the families of both neighborhoods had either come to America via Holland or were of Dutch ancestry.

Even though the Dutch government surrendered all of its interests in what is now the United States to Great Britain in 1664, its cultural influence lasted long after that in the Hudson Valley, particularly in remote frontier settlements. For example, the religious affairs of the people who lived here were attended to by the Dutch Reformed Church, which was the only church in the community until after 1800. Services were said in both English and Dutch until the 1790s. Over time, the names of Anglo-Dutch settlers became more Anglicized. Martinus became Martin, Jacobus became James and so on. Construction techniques common in the heavily Dutch-influenced Kingston area were used more than those of the English settlements to the south in New York. The migration of those early Dutch settlers brings us to families who were the early settlers, and who built what was initially known as the Hayne trading post, and later became the Decker Stone House.

THE HAYNE FAMILY

To understand the early history of the Decker stone house, one must first know about the early families who lived there and their respective genealogies. While the genealogical material can be rather dense, oblique reading, it provides a great deal of background in uncovering the story of the house. There are three families associated with the Decker Stone House in the 18th century: the Haynes, Westfalls and Deckers.

Frederick Hayne (1730?-1807), builder of the original Hayne trading post, was born in Germany and emigrated to America from the lowlands of Holland. It is speculated that he may have gone to Philadelphia, then to Sussex County, New Jersey, as did several other German families. There is some evidence to suggest that he was from Leipzig in Germany and his last name may have been spelled Hans or Heins. Not much is known of the Hayne family genealogy or his early life. He married Catherine (also said to be Catharina) Decker (1738-?), the daughter of Magdalena and Peter Decker. The couple had nine children: Margaret (1759-1840), Peter (1760-?), Tobias (?-?), Huldah (1761-?), Frederick (1767-?), Mary (?-?), Hannah (?-?),

Nancy (?-?), and Catherine (?-?).

Tradition has it that Margaret was the first child to be born in what has become known as the Hayne trading post. After living in what is now the Port Jervis area for about fifteen years, Hayne moved to a farm in Wantage, New Jersey in about 1775. After the death of his wife Catherine Decker, he married Temperance Decker *(her relationship to Catherine Decker, if any, is not known)*. He later served as a private in the colonial militia during the American Revolution.

He died in Wantage and his will, dated January 27, 1807, shows his estate was valued at $939.50. By this instrument he left his second wife "her good feather bed" and all of the furniture. However, he also required that if she remarried, her support from his estate would cease. To his sons he left two shares each of his estate, and to his daughters he left one share each. Sons Frederick and Tobias were his executors.

THE HAYNE TRADING POST

The history of Fort Decker prior to 1798 is a murky one and filled with conjecture. When Frederick Hayne, the builder of a trading post on the site now occupied by the Decker stone building, and his family arrived is not known. Nor is it known when they acquired the property. It was acquired either by negotiations with any remaining Native Americans, or from some of the early settler families, Minisink Patent owners, the New Jersey Proprietors or their successors. Hayne may have even leased the property, or rented from one of the pioneer families; no property deed has been found prior to 1798.

Generally, an individual or family coming into an undeveloped area might just pick a spot, settle down, and create a homestead. Or, they might be given some land by local Native Americans. This was particularly true if the individual had a valued skill. William Tietsoort (Titsworth), the first European to settle in the Neversink Valley, had such skills, as he was a blacksmith. This ability to make tools was sought after by the native peoples.

In the years that followed, patent holders, who were allies

of the Crown, were granted vast tracts of unsettled land in unmapped and uncharted regions. They, in turn, had to negotiate with the local Indian tribes for complete ownership. When the patent holders began surveying these large tracts they would often find squatters on their properties. Many times they let the early settlers stay rather than confronting or evicting them, in large part because the tracts were so vast and stretched over thousands of acres.

In the case of the Neversink Valley, a large land patent was granted in 1704 called the Minisink Patent. The Minisink Patent covered much of what is now western Orange County and the southwestern corner of Sullivan County. The only exception from this patent was the land that had been awarded in the Peenpack Patent to the Cuddebacks, Swartwouts, Van Inwegens and Gumaers in the Upper Neighborhood.

The most immediate need for all of the early settlers was to build some kind of shelter. A primitive structure with a bark roof, dirt floors and log walls might have been built quickly near the site. The chimney may have been made of mud and sticks. Soon after, a more substantial stone structure was often built.

Frederick Hayne arrived in the Delaware Valley some time after 1755, and it is believed the original structure he built on the site was constructed sometime between 1755 and 1760. By the time he arrived, much of the area had been claimed, and a small number of settlers had created a patchwork of farms along the Delaware and Neversink Rivers.

A 1902 newspaper article on the history of the building said: "The structure occupies the site of a fort or blockhouse built some time anterior to the Revolutionary War. . ." The

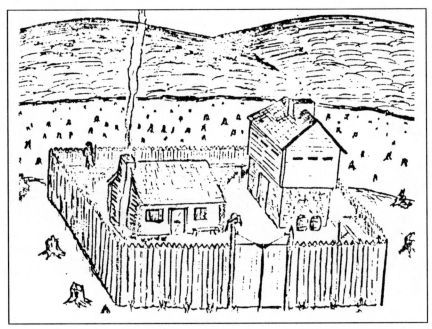

Courtesy Mead Stapler

This is one interpretation of what the structure built by Frederick Hayne may have looked like. A cleared field and a stockade surround a building, right of center, described as a "stone first story and a log second story."

Hayne trading post was described by another nineteenth century author, who had interviewed someone who had first-hand knowledge of the building, as being a blockhouse one and a half stories high. He said that the first half story was constructed of stone and the second story was constructed of logs, with river mud used for mortar. The author goes on to say the original roof was made of small intertwined saplings, covered by larger saplings, and then filled with mud, dirt and gravel, and ultimately covered with a thick coating of river clay. Loopholes were located throughout the building, and served a defensive purpose as slots for rifles; they also provided ventilation and light.

Courtesy Minisink Valley Historical Society

The Hayne trading post and tavern may have looked similar to this view of a typical tavern of the period.

This construction technique used a crude medieval style which secured the building against the elements, and provided some protection from attacks. There is some speculation the present-day basement of the Decker stone house is actually the first floor of the original trading post, and that it was incorporated into the rest of the structure after 1793.

The building served as a tavern and trading place, and the Hayne family probably carried on a trade with the Native Americans. The "blockhouse" was also used as an unofficial military post where settlers could gather for protection. It was said to be one of the most well-built houses in the area. Its location was ideal, in the middle of a fertile valley near the Delaware

River. Open fields with a wide view of the flatland surrounding it made it easily defendable. While these sorts of structures provided early warning posts for farmers and settlers, historians of that period do not believe that they were effective in warding off attacks. Indians did not normally attack fortified houses by themselves. It was only when they were supported by whites did they join in those attacks.

It is not clear whether the trading post was the site of any major military activity during the French and Indian War (1754-1763), when frontier violence occurred regularly. Residents of the area were evacuated, on occasion, to areas north and east of present-day Port Jervis including Rochester, Wawarsing and Old Paltz, where they had relatives and felt more secure.

THE WESTFALL AND DECKER FAMILIES

The second family associated with the Decker stone house in the eighteenth century is the Westfalls. Wilhelmus Westfall married one of Frederick Hayne's daughters, and Fort Decker was sometimes described as Fort Westfall because of this Westfall connection. Believed to have been born in 1753, Wilhelmus Westfall (1753-1796) was baptized on July 8, 1753. His parents, Simeon Westfall (1721-1805) and Jannetje Westbrook (1720-?) were married in 1743. They lived at the eastern end of Machackemeck, present-day Port Jervis, probably near the present-day Machackemeck Churchyard, where they are also buried. Another son by Simeon and Jannetje's marriage, Simeon, built the stone house that stands in Matamoras, Pennsylvania, which also served as a fort during the 18th century. It is now known by an incorrect name, Fort Matamoras.

Wilhelmus Westfall married Margaret Hayne (1759-1840) in either June 1778 or 1780. By this marriage there were ten children: Cathrina (c. 1780 - ?), Alice (or Althe) (c. 1781), Lydia (c. 1783 - ?), David (c. 1789-?), Elizabeth (c. 1791 -?), Apollonia (c. 1792 - ?), Benjamin (c. 1794 - ?), Nancy (c. 1795 - ?), John (c.

Courtesy William Clark

The home of Simeon Westfall, c. 1880, on First Street in Matamoras, Pennsylvania, still stands overlooking the Delaware River.

1795 - ?), and James (c. 1795 - ?). His daughter, Alice (or Althe), is said to be his first child born in the stone house, and she later married Peter Decker. Because of this information we can presume the Westfalls lived in the stone house at some point, although the dates are not clear. It has also been said the Westfalls operated a river ferry near the stone house, where present-day Ferry Street is now located in Port Jervis, just a short walk from Fort Decker.

Sometime after 1783 or 1784, Wilhelmus and Margaret Westfall moved to a farm along the Papakating Creek in Wantage Township, Sussex County, New Jersey. When he died on October 26, 1796, his estate, determined from a will probated December 2, 1796, totaled 511 pounds, 16 shillings and three pence. The administrators were his wife and Peter Hayne, who was probably her brother, and Samuel Decker, all of whom resided in Wantage, and John Salmon of Newton, New Jersey.

Wilhelmus' widow remarried on February 8, 1805 to Noah Terry, a farmer from Wantage, New Jersey. Terry died October 12, 1815. After his death, Margaret, through the efforts of friends, applied in 1839 for a pension for Westfall's Revolutionary War military service. As part of the deposition process she had her sister Huldah Lewis prepare the affidavit because, by that time, Margaret Hayne Westfall Terry had lost her eyesight and was unable to sign the form.

The third family associated with the stone house and for whom it is named, the Deckers, came to the area like so many early settlers, first traveling across the Atlantic from the Netherlands, then up the Hudson River to Kingston, or Esopus as it was known. They made their way south along the Old Mine Road, following the course of present-day Route 209, sometimes settling for a generation in Kingston or south of Kingston, and then to the fertile fields of the Neversink Valley. A Dutch-English dictionary defines the name Decker as meaning to cover decks, or paraphrased, the laying of roofs on houses, or decks on ships.

The family's history and genealogy can be confusing and, because of the lack of records, it is impossible to be sure if it has been recorded accurately and completely. The late Admiral Benton Weaver, a Decker family genealogist and author of **The Decker Genealogy: Some Descendants of the Dutch Immigrants, Johannes (Decker) and Jan Broersen (Decker)** has proposed the following lineage for Martinus Decker; much of this has been confirmed by subsequent research from other sources. He believed the original Decker to settle in the Neversink Valley was Jan Gerretsen (Decker) who came from

Heerden, Gelderland, Holland, sometime in the late 1600s. Born before 1640, he died in 1717, and may be buried in the Machackemeck Churchyard on East Main Street in Port Jervis. Researchers suggest that Jan Decker may have been a councillor of state under Governor General Peter Stuyvesant.

Jan Decker traveled back and forth between Holland and America. According to regional historian Charles Stickney, he owned property in Mombaccus in Ulster County which he purchased in 1685, and sold at an undetermined time to Teunis Oosterhout. He was married in March 1664 to Greitjen Hendricks Westercamp (1642-?) in Esopus, New York (now Kingston). By their marriage there were six children, three of whom are known to have lived near Port Jervis: Johannes (1675-1754), Hendrick (? -?) and Jennetje (? - ?). At least one child lived in Ulster County *(which then took in some of present-day Orange and Sullivan Counties)*, and the other two lived in Wantage and Walpack, New Jersey. As with so much of the region's early history, very little is known about these first two generations.

Martinus Decker is descended from Johannes, one of Jan Gerretson Decker's children, who lived in the present-day town of Deerpark. Johannes was born in 1675, and moved to this area where he died in 1754. He married Hilletjen Kwik (Quick) (?-?) on July 1, 1722, and by this marriage there was at least one child: Sara (1723- ?). Another child, Peter (1711-1773), said to be from this marriage, was an important figure in the region's early history. He has created problems for genealogists because his lineage is not clear; it has been suggested that he may have been adopted by Johannes Decker because at his baptism in 1711 no father was listed, only his mother, Hilletjen Kwik. Benton

Courtesy Minisink Valley Historical Society

Several samples of children's handwriting were found during renovations in the 1980s at Fort Decker including this one located behind the mantlepiece on the second floor. They may date from the Decker era.

Courtesy Minisink Valley Historical Society

The Decker, Westfall and Hayne families, along with most of the other set-tlers worshiped in this Reformed Church that was known as the "haystack." It is believed that the building stood in the back northern cor-ner of the Machackemeck Church burying ground located on East Main Street at the junction with Jersey Avenue. It was burned by Joseph Brant during his raid in 1779.

Weaver and William J. Coulter, a prominent regional genealogist, disagree on this. Weaver believes he is the natural-born son of Johannes. Coulter believes he was adopted. Given the accepted birth date of Peter Decker, it would appear Coulter is right.

Peter married Magdalena Oosterhout (?-?) in 1729 or, as other genealogies suggest, in 1732 or 1733. Records indicate she was baptized November 12, 1710, in Kingston, New York. She was the daughter of Kryn and Marytjen Schut. By Peter Decker's marriage to Magdalena there were nine children: Martinus (1733-1802), Maria (1736-?), Catrina or Catherine (1738-?), Josias (1740-?), Hendricks (1743-?), Annatje (1745-?), Helena (1747-?), Samuel(1749-?), and Joseph (?-?).

It has been documented that Peter Decker, Martinus Decker's father, was in the Port Jervis area as early as 1737, and he probably grew to adulthood here. His name appears in the Minutes of the Precinct of Minisink in 1738, and again in 1739 when an assessment of the Precinct of Minisink to pay for a courthouse in Goshen was made. The listing shows a Petris Decker which is presumably Peter Decker. Church records indicate he was one of the founders of the Dutch Reformed Church organized in Port Jervis in 1737.

There is some disagreement as to the date Peter moved to what is now Sussex County, New Jersey -- in the 1730s or early 1740s -- and settled along the Papakating, a branch of the Wallkill River. He was the founder of the settlement that became Deckertown *(the name was changed in 1902 to Sussex)*. Here he built a log cabin where he lived until he died. As to the exact location of the cabin, again, historians and writers disagree. One puts his home at the present-day location of 29 Hamburg Avenue, another on Main Street near the former Crisman's Hotel, or near the junction of the Port Jervis Turnpike (Main Street) and Newton Street. A small memorial plaque, now covered by brush, is located at the corner of Sussex and Main Streets, and commemorates the spring which is said to be where the log cabin was situated. A block of stone, engraved with a "PD 1749" can be found in the foundation of a house located at 29 Hamburg Avenue.

Because Peter Decker's properties were in proximity to the demarcation line separating the colonies of East and West Jersey and New York, he became embroiled in the largest of all the colonial boundary disputes. He was a farmer but also assisted an area surveyor making surveys. Decker was appointed a Justice of the Peace by King George beginning in 1754; he served until his death. The surveyors of highways met at his house to lay out a road to the Minisink mountains. A businessman, he acquired land, and erected mills in several locations near and around Port Jervis and Deckertown.

Peter Decker must have been involved with military activities during the French and Indian War because as a justice he had a role in the recognition of the courage of a young boy who killed Captain Armstrong. Armstrong was a leader of a branch of the Delaware Indians, who had killed settlers. Decker took Armstrong's scalp to Perth Amboy, New Jersey, the headquarters of the East Jersey Proprietors as proof; the boy received an award and money for his actions. We also know a little about Decker's physical stature; he was considered an able man, and from court testimony, he was said to be a large, strong man. Intelligent and cautious, he could write, as evidenced by his signature on documents.

He died in 1773 in Wantage, New Jersey, and when his will was probated in 1774, his estate was worth L203.S18.D9. He had thirteen horses, twenty cattle, twelve sheep, two hatchets, one pocket compass and a "half a law book." Sons Martinus and Joseph were the executors.

Of the children of Magdalena and Peter we know little. Helena, the youngest daughter, was apparently physically handicapped in some way because in his will, her father left money for her to be managed by the executors. Catherine was married to Frederick Hayne, the builder of the trading post. Son Samuel has been written about to some degree because of the prominence he later achieved in Sussex County. But, he has also created problems for researchers because several men had the same name and may be related.

Of Martinus Decker, we also know relatively little. For example, it is not known where Martinus Decker was born, although Esopus (present-day Kingston) has been suggested as one location. Another possibility is in the Port Jervis area; because we know so little about his father's family, all of this is speculative. He was born November 20, 1733, and was baptized January 20, 1734, in the Dutch Reformed Church in Kingston. Because there was no full-time minister at Machackemeck at the time, his family may have returned to have him baptized in Kingston, as was the tradition. For Martinus' baptism, Pieter La Bonte and Gristjen Osterhout stood as witnesses. His sister Maria was baptized in Kingston on May 18, 1736. His younger sisters and brothers were all baptized later in the Minisink Reformed Church in Montague, New Jersey.

There are two writers who described Martinus Decker's genealogy very differently from Benton Weaver's. An article in **Old Deerpark Days**, an in-house publication for the Reformed Dutch Church of Deerpark and written by S. W. Mills in 1902 stated that Martinus was actually descended from Johannes (or John) Decker who may have been, according to Benton Weaver, actually his grandfather. Or they may be confusing him with another Johannes Decker who also had a son Martinus. Peter Gumaer, in his **History of Deerpark**, also suggested that Martinus was born to John Decker and his wife, whose name he could not recall. A third writer, Professor John Dolph, in presenting a history of the stone house at a ceremony in 1908, also made the same assertion about Martinus' lineage. Dolph suggests that Martinus was born in 1737.

There is another Martinus Decker listed in the Dutch Church records that show his father as Johannes and his mother as Lenas. While no additional genealogical data can be found about this particular Martinus, this author believes that Coulter, Gumaer and Dolph may all be referring to the same man, but a different person than the subject of this book, who also happened to be related to the builder of the stone house.

Other writers have continued this genealogical error in their histories of the building, which makes it more confusing for readers with no detailed knowledge of the family genealogy. In fairness to the earlier genealogists, the information they had access to was not comprehensive and was not as available. In many cases the genealogists may have been relying on oral traditions, which can be inaccurate. In the case of Peter Gumaer, he said as much when explaining how he had come by his information.

We do know that Peter Decker and his family moved to the farm that once made up present-day Sussex. Presumably young Martinus lived here until he got married, and then moved back to the Decker land holdings in Port Jervis in 1760. The first time it can be determined that Martinus Decker was living in

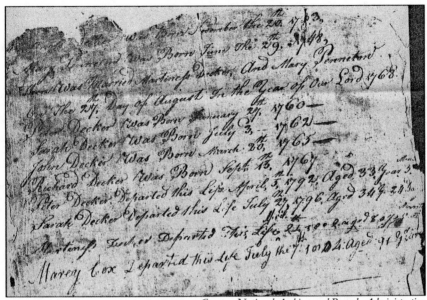

Courtesy National Archives and Records Administration

This page of the family Bible, that includes the genealogical information on Martinus Decker's family, may be in Decker's hand. The page is part of the Revolutionary War Pension application of Decker's second wife. It is now located in the National Archives in Washington, D.C.

Orange County again was in 1775 when he signed a pledge to support the colonials' cause in their disputes with Great Britain.

Church records show Martinus was married twice, first to Jenneke Westbrook (1747-1768?) of Wantage, New Jersey. *(Another source says she was from Woodburn, New York.)* If the records are correct, Decker was twenty-six and his wife would have been thirteen although that seems rather young even by the standards of the day. Jenneke Westbrook was born on September 23, 1747, and baptized in 1748. Her parents were Johannes Dirck Westbrook (1709-?) and Sara Tack (1704-?); she had four siblings. Jenneke bore Martinus four children: Peter

(1760-1792), Sara (1762-1796), John (1765-1843) and Richard (1767-1851). Jenneke probably died in 1767 or 1768, perhaps from complications of childbirth. Not long after her death, with four young children to care for, Martinus Decker married Mary Pennenton (1748-1840) who was born on June 29, 1748. They were married on August 27, 1768, and the ceremony was performed by the Rev. Mancinus of the local Dutch church. At the time of their marriage Martinus was thirty-five years old and Mary was twenty. By this marriage there was one son, Martin (1770-1829?).

A 1790 census shows Martinus Decker's household consisted of three free white males aged sixteen years and older, two free white males under the age of sixteen, and three free white females, including the head of household. Neither Martinus nor Peter's family had slaves.

Decker would have kept many of the Dutch traditions including speaking Dutch and English. There are no images of him nor any physical description - whether he was tall or short,

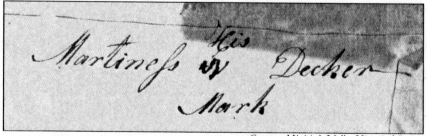

Courtesy Minisink Valley Historical Society

There is only one known document bearing the mark of Martinus Decker and it is affixed to a 1798 deed in the Minisink Valley Historical Society's collection. At this time Decker would have been sixty-five years old and may have been infirmed.

or what color his hair and his eyes were. We can presume he was a hardy man who physically toiled in the fields, and who lived much of his life in the outdoors. Because of the size of his land-holdings he and his father must have been successful business-men. With his journeys between Orange and Sussex Counties, Decker may have been more well-traveled than most men of his time.

It is presumed Martinus could write because he was an officer in the militia. As a lieutenant he would have been required to file daily morning reports providing an accounting of his men, which he would have had to write. A page from the family Bible has the genealogical information listed, and it may well be his handwriting. However, a 1798 deed in the possession of the Society only shows "his mark" on the signature line. The deed was prepared at a time when he would have been sixty-five years old, he may have suffered from some infirmity. We know he was a religious man, that he attended church regularly and served as an elder of the Dutch Reformed Church. His will opens with an unusual affirmation of his religious beliefs.

He signed the pledge of association in 1775, which indi-cates his underlying faith in freedom and liberty, at the very ear-liest of moments in the colonists' bid for freedom. His commit-ment to the cause was strong and dedicated, and his military service, which is extensive, is well documented in his wife's application for a pension in 1839. He does not seem to have ever wavered in his revolutionary fervor.

One of the most interesting things we know about him was his personal motto - "Perseverance and Vigilance." The harshness of living on the frontier, and having been involved in

Courtesy Peter Osborne

Martinus Decker's original tombstone was lost to the ravages of time and this twentieth century headstone marks his final resting place.

three military and civil conflicts of the eighteenth century would seem to represent the values of those words. He came home from the Revolutionary War and lived an honorable and active life, participating in church and civic affairs, not unlike someone who might have been a hero to him - George Washington.

Martinus Decker died April 24, 1802, and was buried less than one hundred feet from where he worshiped in the Machackemeck Churchyard, and within sight of his large land holdings. The churchyard was across the road from Cole's Fort, where a senior citizen complex is now located (2007), on the corner of East Main Street and Jersey Avenue. A friend wrote upon his passing: "He was an upright man and died a Christian and at the time of his death was an Elder in the Church at Deerpark." After his demise it was said Martinus Decker was beloved and lamented by those who knew him. When his will was probated he first and foremost took care of his wife, and then divided his property among his sons. With his passing at the age of 69, an important piece of the community's fabric was lost, as well as a piece of its early history.

As late as 1907, fragments of Decker's headstone were still visible along with his daughter Sarah's headstone, who was buried nearby, close to the boundary of St. Mary's Catholic Cemetery. According to a 1969 MVHS newsletter his gravestone read: "1733 Martinus Decker departed this life April 24, 1802." The ravages of time have destroyed the old stone. The grave now has a marker that was placed there by the Daughters of the Revolution, an organization, now defunct, that honored the service of the men and women of the Revolution. Four years after the death of Martinus, his wife, Mary, married John Middaugh on June 5, 1806 in Wantage, New Jersey. She died in 1840.

Another important allied family that played a role in the development of the large Decker land holdings was the Caskey family. They were closely tied to the Deckers by the 1781 marriage of Martinus' daughter Sarah to Samuel Caskey (?-1833), who owned a large farm adjacent to the Decker farm on the west. The earliest citation for the Caskey family living in the area is in 1775 when they are listed in Minisink Precinct records.

Life On The Frontier

Once a shelter was constructed the land was cleared and crops planted. The size of the Hayne/Decker property is not known. To the east lay the Shawangunk Ridge, to the north, the southeastern edge of the Appalachian plateau, and to the south, the Delaware River. The property was certainly an attractive one; as the years passed, land for crops was cut out from woodland. Nearby tracts of forests allowed for the cutting of wood and hunting of game.

Grains provided flour, and corn, beans, carrots, turnips and pumpkins were all planted as well. These crops could be stored to provide food during the winter. Typically, a family had a team of horses and oxen, a few milk cows, a hog or two, chickens, ducks and geese (as much for their feathers as for the meat).

Easily obtained water from the Delaware, dug wells or springs were a necessary commodity, and it has been suggested that there was a cistern in the basement of Fort Decker, although archaeological excavations have not uncovered it to date. A nineteenth century newspaper article describes a community well that was across the street in the current Port Jervis

Memorial Rose Garden, and
located approximately where
the flagpole is today (2006).
The Delaware River was also
several hundred feet from the
building. This may have been
the original water source for
the families that lived on the
site. An outhouse or "necessary" was some distance from
the building, and provided the
family with its sanitary needs.

One final feature of
the property that is not so evi-
dent today, but would have
been to its occupants, was its

Courtesy Rick Hibberd

lovely setting. One can imagine what the fields spread out in
front of the building looked like late in the summer with the
Shawangunk ridge off in the distance, and the Delaware River
passing nearby and visible at the turn where it meets the
Neversink River. There would have been an idyllic quality to living in the valley long before there were thousands of people living here.

Most activities of those early settlers in the 1700s were
focused towards survival, and preparing for the future. Whether
it was the growing of grains and corn, livestock, the production
and preservation of food, or creating clothing and household
items like candles, furniture or supplies, their days were filled
with work.

A family's survival was dependent on its members doing their share of work. Large families provided the labor necessary for the myriad of tasks. Until the conclusion of the American Revolution, most of the local farms were self-sufficient, purchasing items like sugar, spices, seasoning and finished goods from itinerant traders. After 1800 trade goods became more available and common; life became somewhat easier for those living in the stone house. Cooking demonstrations that are conducted today at Fort Decker reveal how challenging it was for the women of the household to manage the daily needs of large families.

Courtesy Peter Osborne

The family's vegetable garden was a major source of food for early settlers. Vegetables that were grown included turnips, carrots, beets, pumpkins, peas and beans, all of which could be stored through the winter months.

Courtesy Fort Delaware

After young people did their chores, like getting water, milking the family cow, feeding the chickens, keeping the fires going, cleaning the stalls or dipping candles they were able to play with homemade toys. There was not the sense of leisure as we know it today.

A GENERATION OF SUFFERING:
THE FRENCH AND INDIAN WAR AND
THE WAR FOR INDEPENDENCE

Fort Decker was witness to two major military conflicts of the eighteenth century: the French and Indian War (1754-1763) and the American Revolution (1775-1783). Also, there was the fight between the colonies of East and West Jersey and New York over a large triangular-shaped piece of land that was thousands of acres in size. This was known as the Border War (1719-1774); it was the largest of all the colonial land disputes.

The occupants of the stone house played a role in all three events. The three decades between 1755 and 1785 were "indeed the times that tried men's souls," as one writer put it in the years leading up to America's war for independence. George Fluhr, the Pike County Historian, has written that the generation of people who lived on the frontier during the last half of the 18th century was the "generation of suffering." So it was for the Hayne, Westfall, and Decker families, and all the valley families who lived through these dramatic times.

With only a few periods of peace, settlers lived in fear of raids, initially by local Native Americans who, after being pushed westward, came back to attack with a vengeance. Then, in the

American Revolution, it was the British, the Loyalists, and their Native American allies from upper New York State who attacked the settlements along the Delaware.

It is not clear whether Fort Decker was the site of any major military activity during the French and Indian War. No sources indicate that it was although it was situated in a strategic location. It is also not known if any of the Hayne, Westfall or Decker men were involved in any militia action, although it seems probable they were.

During the war, it is believed there were three forts in the lower neighborhood, although only one can be identified with certainty. Cole's Fort was built in present-day Port Jervis, then within the colony of East Jersey, at the junction of today's East Main Street and Jersey Avenue. Today the site is occupied by a senior housing project (2007). This Fort, directly across the road

Courtesy Minisink Valley Historical Society

from the Dutch church and graveyard, was home to Wilhelmus Cole, and was said to have been built by the New Jersey Frontier Guards. No information survives that describes whether or not it saw any action as a fort.

During the French and Indian War several raids were made into the area, and residents were evacuated to areas north and east of present-day Port Jervis, to Rochester, Wawarsing and Old Paltz, where many settlers had relatives and would have been more secure. Raids also occurred in Sussex County, and several are documented in James Snell's **History of Sussex and Warren Counties, New Jersey**, although none mentions Fort Decker. This era of the building's history is rather murky. What has been written of that period seems to indicate that Hayne traded regularly with local Native Americans. From that, one can conclude that the trading post was not attacked, at least not by locals.

Another difficult period for these families and the landowners of the region was a heated dispute that has been described as the Border War. The dispute occurred among the colonies of East Jersey, West Jersey and New York, and lasted from 1719 until its final resolution in 1774. This dispute was the largest colonial land dispute in America, and dragged on through the courts and various legislatures for six decades. Not only did settlers have to struggle to survive and fight off attacks during the French and Indian War, but they also had to fight claims and cross-claims for lands they thought they had purchased from patent holders who had been granted the land by the monarchy. The old "Jersey Claim Line" can still be found on maps of the region.

The Hayne/Westfall/Decker farm was clearly below the Jersey Claim line as established in 1719. One might presume that they were "Jerseymen." However, New York claimed a peninsula-shaped piece of land that extended down the Delaware River to Minisink Island, south of Montague. This is clearly shown on a 1765 map that was made by the Minisink Patent holders. Peter Decker's name appears in Precinct of Minisink minutes in 1738 and 1739, so that would indicate they considered themselves "Yorkers," at least at that point in time.

Peter Decker, Martinus' father, however, moved from the Port Jervis area to what is now Sussex, to a property located along the Papakating Brook, a branch of the Wallkill River. Here the senior Decker also found himself embroiled in the boundary dispute, as he was concerned with the legitimacy of his property's title. Soon he found himself involved with some of the major figures of the boundary dispute including James Alexander, the Surveyor-General of the Jerseys; Decker's name appears in the minutes of the New Jersey Proprietors. In 1745 Peter Decker executed his lease with the proprietors of East Jersey and, like everyone else, waited for a line to be run that would divide New York from New Jersey, which did not happen until 1769.

Through these years Peter Decker served as a chain bearer for surveyor Richard Gardiner. It was during his service as a chain bearer that he was involved with another of the major figures in the boundary dispute, Colonel Thomas DeKay. DeKay was an officer in the Orange County militia, who lived near present-day New Jersey State Route 94 on the current boundary line. DeKay threatened anyone near him who claimed any land for

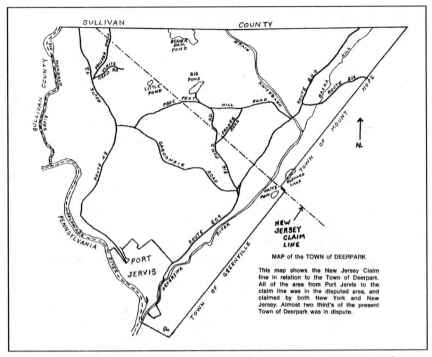

MAP of the TOWN of DEERPARK

This map shows the New Jersey Claim
line in relation to the Town of Deerpark.
All of the area from Port Jervis to the
claim line was in the disputed area, and
claimed by both New York and New
Jersey. Almost two third's of the present
Town of Deerpark was in dispute.

Courtesy Minisink Valley Historical Society

The Jersey Claim line was the focus of much anguish, fighting, legal skirmishes and a border war.

New Jersey. Analysis has shown that DeKay's farm was actually six miles into New Jersey, and Peter Decker was fourteen miles into the province, based on pre-settlement lines. In July, 1753 Peter Decker was involved in a fight as a survey of the Sussex County boundary line was being conducted.

Decker was witness to a physical fight that occurred between Richard Gardiner, the surveyor, John Herring, another chain bearer, and the sons of Thomas DeKay. The first two were beaten by DeKay's sons. Decker offered no assistance to Gardiner or Herring, and during later court proceedings his lack of involvement was duly noted and at the bottom of the deposition he signed his name.

In 1754 Peter Decker was part of a team that apprehended Jacobus Swartwout of Huguenot for "a riot committed by him and others in the county of Sussex." New Yorkers would later call it a kidnapping. This was done in retaliation for an earlier action similar in nature undertaken by Swartwout. Decker would also be arrested by DeKay at some point, and was released after the intervention of James Alexander.

Because all their documented military service took place after 1774, and whatever military records exist start at that time, it cannot be determined on which side of the dispute they stood. Because they owned land on both sides of the line, they certainly would have wanted to see the line settled. At least one deed from 1712 describes land owned by Simon Westphalia (or Westfall) as being within the Western Division of the Province of New Jersey. This was located in an area that is believed to be within or near present-day Port Jervis.

The Border War era was a time of cross claims, land grabbings, kidnappings, incarceration of officials on both sides of the line, and lawsuits. Even during the survey of the region by representatives of all three colonies in 1719 to settle the issue, one of the Decker family's fields of crops was burned to the ground by Yorkers claiming the land was theirs. The map shown illustrates the dimension of the problem for local residents. Tax collectors and militia commanders from both colonial governments tried to get service and taxes out of each individual.

A commission was finally appointed in 1769 by the King of England, and after five years of hearings, surveys, discussions and meetings, the line was finally determined to be where it is today. With the marking of the boundary in 1774, the Hayne/Westfall/Decker farm was clearly on the New York side of the border.

The American Revolution closely followed the conclusion of the boundary dispute. It also brought out the strongest of passions in people who lived in the region, who either supported independence or the King of England. The stakes were important, and whatever one's position, it was fraught with danger. That was true in the Minisink. John Adams, a major figure in the American War for Independence, and our nation's second President, later wrote in the years following the war with Britain that "We were about one third Tories, one third timid and one

Courtesy Minisink Valley Historical Society

The gathering clouds of the rebellion against the British King extended to the frontier, where militias were created and forts built.

third true blue."

Fort Decker and its occupants were the focal point of a number of historic events that occurred between 1776 and 1783. As tensions flared between the British and colonists, a number of military forts were constructed by the colonies of New York and New Jersey. Some houses in the Delaware River valley were heavily fortified, including several within the present-day limits of the City of Port Jervis and the town of Deerpark. They included Cole's Fort (East Main Street), a blockhouse owned by Peter Kuykendall (Broome Street), Major Decker's Fort, (Neversink Drive, Huguenot) sometimes confused with Fort Decker, Fort Van Auken (Spring Street, near Port Jervis Country Club), Westfall Fort (Huguenot), Fort Gumaer (Godeffroy), Fort Depuy (Godeffroy), Fort Dewitt (Godeffroy) and Fort Westbrook (Westbrookville). It is believed that most of the fortifications were erected in 1777 or 1778.

There are surviving accounts of what these forts looked like. A description of at least one of the French and Indian War-era forts, Fort Gardner, near Gardnerville, New York, survives. It is described as a wooden dwelling house with five log houses palisaded in a 100-foot square. Dimensions of two other nearby fortified houses have passed down through history. The first, Cole's Fort, was built by the colony of New Jersey in 1755 to provide protection for local colonists during the French and Indian War. It has been described as a home that was a wooden dwelling 60 x 23 feet, which would make it substantially longer than Fort Decker but less deep. In addition, there were two small blockhouses all enclosed within a square stockade that measured about 120 feet on each side. Presumably Cole's Fort was rebuilt or reinforced after the beginning of hostilities with Great Britain. Major Johannes Decker's fortified house, located on Horn Road, was described as a "house . . . of logs surrounded by wooden fortifications."

While some fortified buildings used stone walls, most used wood because of its availability. A trench was dug between three and six feet deep and posts that could be between fifteen to eighteen feet high and a foot in diameter were sharpened at one end and placed vertically with a horizontal stringer tying them together. One of the challenges for the commanders was the maintenance of the structures, because wood begins to decompose in five years.

Courtesy Minisink Valley Historical Society

Fort Delaware in Narrowsburg, New York, is a reconstructed French and Indian War-era military fortification. Fort Decker may have been similar in appearance.

Courtesy Minisink Valley Historical Society

Logs were placed vertically in a trench to create the outer perimeter of a fortification.

As historian Mildred Parker Seese wrote in her book **Old Orange Houses**, "every substantial house was a potential fort," and "most stone houses did serve as a fort at one time or another." When Joseph Brant, who played a significant role in the region's military history, described his incursions into the valley in 1778 and 1779, he said that there "were many forts about the place, into which they (the colonists) were always ready to run like groundhogs."

There is much interest in what Fort Decker looked like in this era and also what the entire fortified structure may have looked like. However, to date, no pictures or drawings have been found. It is not known for certain how large the Fort Decker compound was, or if it included other buildings. Was it just one building surrounded by a log palisade, or was it a larger compound with several buildings that could provide protection for a number of families and for assigned militia men? It is known that Fort Decker, while not an official military installation, was fortified when tensions between Great Britain and the colonies reached the breaking point.

Several pension applications of militia men who served at Fort Decker during the Revolution give us tantalizing snippets of information as to what the compound looked like. The pension application of Martin Cuykendall, a private in the Orange County militia, stated that he worked "at a small piquet fort called Fort Decker in 1777." Piquet is a French word that means "post, stake, or picket." The most significant description of what Fort Decker looked like comes from Benjamin Davis, who described the compound as "the stockade at Martinus Decker's settlement." A third applicant, James Burt, was "stationed a part of this time at the stockade of Martinus Decker's settlement."

William Knapp, another militia man, stated that he had served for weeks at "Martinus Decker's fort in Minisink." Richard Clark describes part of his military service as being at "Martinus Decker's Fort." Moses Knapp, stationed at the Fort in May 1779, said that during his time forty men were garrisoned there. A much later description comes from a 1969 MVHS newsletter that says the (Hayne) trading post and other buildings were destroyed in the 1779 raid by Joseph Brant.

From these descriptions we can probably make several assumptions. The first is that Martinus Decker's settlement consisted of a number of buildings, including several residences,

barns and outbuildings. Also, that some, perhaps all were surrounded by a stockade of logs. Finally, we can assume that the
militia who were stationed there either stayed within the con-
fines of the stockade or outside its walls but close enough to
retreat inside in the event of an attack. Today when one views
Fort Decker he is only seeing one building in what was a setting
of several.

Another question concerns the disposition of the palisade wall. In the 1890s, a local newspaper article reported part
of the Fort's palisade wall, including old stumps, had been dis-

Courtesy Allan Berner

*When the trolley track and electric lines were being run near Fort Decker
in the closing years of the nineteenth century, stumps were found that were
said to be from the original palisade wall that surrounded Fort Decker.
When the street was repaved in the 1980s, and again in 1999, the rails
were still visible after being uncovered.*

covered near the building as utility poles were being dug. These were similar to stumps found when John Cannon, a later owner of the property, was having the foundation excavated for his house at 125 West Main Street. Well-preserved remains of the old stumps were also found when excavations were made for the trolley track that ran in front of Fort Decker.

More recently, excavations in the street in front of Fort Decker did not locate any remains of the palisade wall. In September, 1999, the City of Port Jervis removed the trolley track along Old West Main Street, and into West Main Street. The author requested the city's Department of Public Works to dig a trench that was four feet deep and approximately the length of the building.

A two-inch layer of blacktop was removed. The trolley rails (four inches in height and five feet, seven inches from rail to rail on the inside) which had been encapsulated, along with the ties, in concrete, at a later date, and ballast for the track, were all removed. After the ballast was removed, at a depth of about fifteen inches, a layer of river-bottom sand was found. At a depth of eighteen inches, a few pieces of ceramic were found; however, there were no soil disturbances down deeper, although several stacked boulders were found directly in front of the porch of the building, also at a depth of about eighteen inches. No post molds or lines of post molds were found in the trench that was dug roughly the length of the building. The soil in the trench was sterile and clear of any artifacts down to about four feet and extending eight feet, eight inches from the curb out to the middle of the street.

Because the trench was only dug out to the middle of the

street (the width of the trolley track) it is quite possible the stockade was farther out, closer to the present-day Port Jervis Memorial Rose Garden. The electric poles seen in photographs of the period show them on both sides of the street, so that may account for the previously mentioned citation. If one accepts the idea that Fort Decker was one of several buildings, then the current structure may have been near one of the walls, part of which was said to have been found by Cannon. The rest of the compound spread out further, perhaps onto West Main Street and down Old West Main Street.

Life in these fortified houses was difficult. The buildings were hot in the summer and cold in the winter. Even today, snow is occasionally found in corners of Fort Decker during a windy snowstorm. The buildings were fire hazards during the summer. The area around the Fort was probably muddy during wet weather because of poor drainage; there were probably large pools of stagnant water nearby. Supplies were difficult to come by, especially at outposts like Fort Decker. Sickness was easily passed on in such close quarters, and of course, there were the pesky flies and mosquitoes.

For a soldier there was guard duty several times a week, transporting of water, cooking, gardening and the tending of animals, as well as construction work on the fort itself. Since there were regular rotations of men coming and going, there was probably constant military activity, including drilling, going on. For families living in these places life was equally difficult, because every time members left the fort to work on crops or to collect livestock it could be the last time. Everyone residing there would have been under a constant state of alert.

Courtesy Minisink Valley Historical Society

From the perspective of two hundred years, the service of the three families, and in particular Martinus Decker is impressive. These were passionate, dramatic and turbulent times, and the end result was not preordained. Military service was probably not new to the Hayne, Westfall or Decker families. The families that lived in the Fort were true patriots and supporters of the cause, both in their military service and in their duty to organizations like the Committee of Safety. When they support- ed the cause of liberty they put their personal safety in jeopardy as well as that of their families and loved ones. The rewards of their hard work - their farms, buildings, herds, and crops - were equally at risk. If patriots were caught by the British they could be hung or imprisoned as traitors, and their properties taken or destroyed by the Crown's forces.

On June 26, 1775, a Committee of Safety and Observation, with John Young as its president, was created just after the first English forts were taken in New York State. Among the names on the document creating the organization were Peter Decker, Martinus Decker, Martinus Decker Jr., Simon and Wilhelmus Westfall. Both Martinus Decker and Martin Decker also signed the Association Pledge for the Precinct of Goshen, Minisink District in September, 1775 as did Wilhelmus Westfall and Simon Westfall.

These men also served in the Orange County militia units and were involved in a number of military engagements. Martinus Decker served in the Third Regiment of the Orange County Militia as a lieutenant, and also in the Second Regiment of the Ulster County Militia. When he was chosen by the Orange County militia in the winter of 1776 to serve as second lieutenant, it reflected the high esteem in which he was held. It seems probable that he also served during the French and Indian War and had been exposed to the hazards of frontier warfare, although no evidence to support this exists. During the Revolution he served under the command of Captain Moses Kortright and Colonel William Allison at various times. He would have also been familiar to Col. John Hathorn, the leader of the American militia units at the Battle at Minisink.

The local militia was typically called out when needed, and kept on active duty as long as necessary. It could be called out of the state for only three months at a time, but in the case of the Orange County unit, the period of service was generally several weeks. Every male between the ages of sixteen and fifty

Courtesy Minisink Valley Historical Society

was enrolled, and in the later years of the Revolution, the age was increased to sixty. Men could fight in different units at different times, and this occurred often. Regular rations of rum, sugar and tea were given, the amount according to rank. A captain's pay was $40 per month; a lieutenant's was $26.

The service of the militia was not always well regarded by General George Washington or his officer corps. Washington was involved in several battles where militia units fled under the onslaught of British regulars. In at least one case they left him alone on a battlefield; militia units did not have the discipline Washington would later require in the regular army. The officers of the militia were generally popular or important men locally, but not necessarily the best leaders or the most courageous. This is not to say the militia did not serve bravely or willingly, but the citizen soldiers were also on temporary duty, not full-time soldiers bound to the army for more than short periods of time. Under the right circumstances they were very much up to the job.

For local men, who had farms to run or businesses to maintain, it was the best way in which they could serve their neighbors, protect their homes, and ultimately make a stand against British rule. Martinus Decker's military service is typical of the valiant service of so many of the militia.

Among the places Lt. Decker served was Fort Montgomery at the eastern end of Orange County, in 1776 and 1777. He was also in New City, New York, and the Ramapo Pass (near Sloatsburg, New York), guarding a strategic pass that if left open would have allowed the British to move their forces into the Hudson Valley. It was here he may have actually seen General George Washington in person. He also served at Morristown and Paramus in New Jersey, and was at Fort Montgomery, overlooking the Hudson River, just days before it was taken by the British in 1777. His unit was discharged just before the dramatic American loss, but was immediately called back into service after the Fort fell to the British.

By 1778, there was such fear of Indian attacks and incursions by the British and their allies on the western frontier of Ulster and Orange Counties, that Decker's company was kept in a constant state of alert. The unit was divided into classes, and one class was always on duty, including scouting parties and guard duty; this arrangement was used until the beginning of

Courtesy Peter Osborne

During archaeological excavations, a Revolutionary War-era coat button and gun flint were found in the test pit excavated near the southwestern corner of Fort Decker where a door had been filled in.

1783. The unit served at a number of locations including "Lt. Martinus Decker's fort," Major Decker's fort, Kuykendall's blockhouse and Van Fleet's fort. Decker's service included the command of Fort Van Auken in Pike County in 1778, where survivors of the battle and massacre at Wyoming stopped after suffering tremendous losses. He also stood guard at local homes during times of alarms.

In August 1778, Fort Decker was the scene of activity that led to a court-martial case. Captain Andrew Miller of the militia unit serving at Fort Decker was charged with leaving his post at the Fort, and going to Major Decker's fort on the Horn Road. Miller presented testimony that his ammunition supplies and food rations were running low, and that he had no choice, a position that the court upheld in its final ruling. As part of the testimony, a scout reported that Brant was said to be coming down the valley to attack the settlement. This impending attack with little food or supplies justified Miller leaving. It is worth noting that in October 1778 Brant did indeed raid the area. Another interesting connection in the trial was that it was administered by Lt. Col. Benjamin Tusten, who was later to be killed at the Battle of Minisink.

Twice Decker's unit was to deal with spies. The first time was in 1777, when they witnessed the hanging of an unidentified spy somewhere along the Hudson River. Then again in 1779, when a rumor of spies in the river valley neighborhood saw Decker's unit go to the Ten Mile River area, in present-day Sullivan County. There they captured two prominent British Loyalist spies. They were former area residents, Edward Hicks

and Robert Land, and both were attempting to get messages to the Indians at Niagara. After their capture, Decker attended their general court-martial in which Land was given the death sentence. Hicks was to be confined for the remainder of the war. The spies were then taken to Count Casimir Pulaski, the famed Polish military officer whose legions served in the Orange County area including Port Jervis.

Finally, in 1782, Decker's unit was called to Wawarsing to deal with attacks made on the settlements there. After 1783, with peace negotiations

Courtesy Minisink Valley Historical Society underway in Europe, Decker's military service came to an end. After his death and upon the application of Martinus Decker's second wife for a military pension from the federal government, his fellow soldiers called him a "valiant officer and always at his post." Another said he was a "good officer and much beloved by soldiers and always ready to do his duty."

There is a Martinus Decker listed as having served in the Fifth Regiment of the Continental Line from New York, although it is not certain if it is the same person who served in the militia and is the subject of this book. A Martin Decker is also listed and some names match other local militia listings but it is not clear if it is the same person.

Peter Gumaer wrote that Decker was "a brave, active and efficient officer whose motto was 'Vigilance and Perseverance,'" and that he was a "sworn enemy of the Tories and Indians." Gumaer also wrote that Decker had not received any pay when he was on duty at Fort Decker. Peter Gumaer was a good friend to Decker, and this interesting fact only adds to the legacy of a true patriot.

Peter Van Auken later testified that his daughter Catherine died in 1778, just after the Battle at Monmouth, and Decker was stationed in command at Fort Van Auken on the Delaware River in Pike County. Decker subsequently supervised her temporary burial and funeral near the fortified building. When the enemy left the region, her body was taken across the river and buried in the Machackemeck Churchyard on East Main Street.

Wilhelmus Westfall's service in the American Revolution was similar to that of Martinus Decker. He enlisted in the early summer of 1776, and his military records indicate he served in many of the same places as Decker. Beginning as a private, by the end of the war he had been promoted to captain of his company. Westfall's father-in-law, Frederick Hayne, whose military records are not available, appears to have served in at least some capacity with the county militia at the beginning of the war.

The full transcription of Martinus Decker's Revolutionary War service, remembered more than fifty years after he had fought the British and Indians, is attested to by his son:

On this sixth day of October 1840 personally appeared before the court of common please being a court of record in and for the County of Sussex and State of New Jersey John Decker a resident of the town of Wantage County of Sussex and State of New Jersey aged Seventy five years who being first duly sworn according to law doth on his oath make the following declaration in order to obtain the benefit of the provisions of the act of Congress passed July the 4th 1836 and the act explanatory of said act passed March the 3d 1837; That he is the son of Martinus Decker who was the husband of Mary Penneton who afterwards was the wife of John Middaugh and who was a widow on the 4 day of July 1836 and who died on the third day of April 1840.

He further declares that he is the only heir that he knows of living of Martinus Decker who was a Lieutenant in the militia of the County of Orange and State of New York That Martinus Decker was chosen by the company of militia under the command of Capt Moses Kortright and the Regiment commanded by Col William Allison in the winter of 1776 Benjamin Thurston was Lieut Colonel and John Decker Major That as he has been informed and believes his father Martinus Decker was called out under Capt Kortright to Fort Montgomery in the month of May or June 1776 and served one month this service was under Col Allison or Clinton.

That he has been informed and believes that the said Martinus Decker after the battle of Long Island was again called out to Fort Montgomery and along the Hudson River and to Ramapoo and Paramus and was out one month in the said service as a Lieutenant under Capt Kortright and under Col Allison this was in August or September 1776.

That in December of the said year Col Allisons Regiment was called out in a body to a place called New City in the county of Orange near the Hudson River Capt Kortrights company was out with the rest of the Regiment and Martinus Decker was out as a Lieutenant in the said company and served with the rest of the Regiment at New City and other places along the Hudson River from in December 1776 until about the twenty fourth of January 1777 and was discharged with the rest of the Regiment at the expiration of a service of Six weeks.

That in the spring of 1777 his father Martinus Decker was again called out to Tappan and other places along the frontiers of New Jersey under he believes Capt Jones and under Col Allison or Cooper and served fifteen days. That in August 1777 Col Allisons Regiment was called out to Fort Montgomery and Capt Kortrights company went with the rest of the Regiment and Martinus Decker went as the Lieutenant of the said company and after they had been there one month the Militia belonging to Col Allisons Regiment was discharged with orders to be ready at the first call in this service Martinus Decker served one month as a Lieutenant .

That immediately after Fort Montgomery was taken Col Allisons Regiment was called out under Col Thurston and Major John Decker to a place called Meurderes Creek on the Hudson River That the Company of Capt Kortright with Martinus as one of the Lieutenants went to Meurderes creek and Joined with the rest of the Regiment at that place and followed the British up the River as far as Bankses Bridge where a part of the men made a stand but he has understood and believes that Lieutenant Decker with a few choice men went as far as Kingston which before they reached it was burnt by the British who had retreated.

That the said Lieutenant Decker was present when the spy was hung who was taken when on his way to meet Gen Burgoyne. After He went to Kingston the company returned to New Windsor and after a service of one month Lieutenant Decker was discharged with the rest of the Regiment This service was done under Lieut Col Thurston and Major John Decker That in the Spring of 1778 the Indians began to make a formidable appearance on the western frontiers of Orange and Ulster Counties and threatened devastation to the whole frontier and the militia on the west side of the mountain was retained at home to guard along the said frontiers.

That the militia was Classed into detachments each detachment doing its duty in turn under the different officers of their respective companies Capt Kortrights company was one of those along the frontier and was retained to guard along the Delaware and Neversink Rivers but this declarant is unable to state with accuracy the different times that Lieutenant Decker was out in service except the following upon alarms and after Spies He has been informed and believes that in June 1778 the come down upon the frontiers in considerable force. Capt Kortrights company was called out to Martinus Deckers fort and served one week upon alarm and Lieutenant Decker served as a Lieutenant in the said Fort one week Col Newkirk or Pawling had command along the frontiers.

That in the month of October of the said year the Indians again made a decent (sic) upon the western frontiers of Orange and Ulster Counties and killed several of the inhabitants this made a general alarm and the militia of the surrounding country was called out Capt Kortrights company was called out to Dewitts fort and served two weeks under Col

Pawling or Newkirk. In this service Lieutenant Decker was out two weeks as a Lieutenant.

That on the 19th (sic) of July 1779 the Indians made a decent (sic) upon Minisink and destroyed the property of the Inhabitants by fire the alarm was given and the militia was called out and followed the Indians to a place called Beaver brook Capt Kortrights company was called out and Lieutenant Decker was out in the said company as a Lieutenant from the time the alarm was given until he was discharged at least two weeks this service was under a part of the time under Col Hathorn and Tusten and the rest of the time was in the Fort called Deckers Fort.

That sometime in the summer of 1780 and while Col Seward of New Jersey had command along the Minisink frontier a report was circulated that there was Tories in the woods of Pennsylvania who assisted the Indians in committing their depredations upon the whites. Capt Kuykendolls of the New Jersey Militia was ordered out with a detachment of men a part of which was taken from Capt Kortrights Company and Martinus Decker went and served as a Lieutenant in the said company in fereting (sic) out the Tories at least one week.

In the spring of 1781 it was reported that spies was in the neighborhood of the Minisink frontier Lieutenant Decker was ordered out with a detachment of fifteen men to catch them they Rendezvoused at Levi Van Ettens and went to the Delaware crossed over to Pennsylvania and went through the woods to a place called Pond Eddy and recrossed to the York side of the River and went up the River to a place called ten mile River where they caught two of the spies named Robert Land and Edward Hicks in this service Martinus Decker served as a Lieutenant commandant for at least one week in June of the said year.

Capt Kortrights company was called out on alarm along the Delaware frontier and served three days in this alarm Lieutenant Decker served three days a Lieutenant That in August or September 1782 the Indians made a decent upon the western frontier of Ulster County and burnt Warwasink Capt Kortrights company was again called out and went to Dewitts fort and served two weeks and was discharged at the expiration of the said term Martinus Decker went with the said company and served in the said company as a Lieutenant for the term of two week under Col Pawling.

He further states that from the nature of the war along the frontier and from personal knowledge of a part of the same he has no doubt but his father Martinus Decker served at least two years as a Lieutenant in the Militia of Orange County He further declares that he served as the second Lieutenant of Capt Kortright and Capt Willhelemus Westfalls company during the whole of the war.

He further declares that his father Martinus Decker was married to Mary Penneton on the 27 day of August Seventeen hundred and Sixty Eight by the Rev Mr Marinus and that the said Martinus Decker died on the 24th day of April Eighteen hundred and two this deponent further saith that he is the son of Martinus Decker by a former wife that the widow of Martinus Decker was afterwards married on the fifth day of June - Eighteen Hundred and six - by the Rev W Van Benschocten in the town of Wantage and State of New Jersey and that to John Middaugh who died on the 22d day of February 1822 and that the said Mary Middaugh remained a widow until her death which happened at the time before stated That the said Mary Middaugh formerly Mary Decker Died without issue and that this This deponent is the son of Martinus Decker by his first wife and that he is the only heir of Martinus Decker that he knows living.

That the accompanying record of the family of Martinus Decker as sworn to by John Decker is a true record of the said family He hereby relinquishes every claim to a pension or annuity except the present and

declares that the name of Martinus Decker or Mary Middaugh is not on
the pension roll of the agency of any State in the Union Sworn and sub-
scribed to the day and year aforesaid.

John Decker

And so ends the pension application of Martinus Decker.
The application ended with the death of John Decker. Martinus
Decker's family never received any compensation, in the form of
a pension, to which they were entitled for his brave war service.
This was not uncommon for the local militia as attested to by
David Van Inwagen in 1847:

On this tenth day of May 1847 personally appeared before the
undersigned a Justice of the peace in and for the said County David Van
Inwagen of the Town of Thompson in the County of Sullivan and State
of New York but now in the town of Deerpark County of Orange and
State aforesaid aged Eighty three years to me known as a man of truth and
veracity who being first duly sworn according to law doth on his Oath depose
and say that he was born and raised to manhood and lived until the last few
years in the valley called Peenpack on the western frontiers of Orange and
Ulster Counties - That during the Revolutionary war this valley was con-
tinually exposed to the depredations of the Indians who infested the moun-
tains and woods west of the valley That the inhabitants were continually
exposed to the scalping knife and tomahawk and several were killed at mid-
day when at work in the fields . . . He is satisfied that from what he knew
of the services of Lieut Martines Decker that he could not have done less
than one year actual service as a Lieutenant during the war This deponent
further saith that he never received any pay for any service that he done nor
does he know of any of those who lived in the valley and served in the mili-

tia that did. He does not believe that Martines Decker received pay for services done on the western frontier of Orange and Ulster Counties - He was well acquainted with the said Decker until his death which took place in April 1802 This deponent was at the burial and saw his remains interred in the old Dutch burying ground near where now is built the village of Port Jervis.

JOSEPH BRANT'S RAIDS OF 1778 AND 1779

Twice, in the fall of 1778 and the summer of 1779, British officer Joseph Brant, his Mohawk allies and British Loyalists raided the Neversink and Delaware Valleys, destroying property and spreading terror among the people who lived there. Brant, the most well-known figure in both raids, was a Mohawk Indian; he was described alternately as a "savage" and a distinguished and educated man. No one disagrees that he was a skilled military leader and tactician. Born south of Lake Erie in Ohio in 1743, his first military experience was at the Battle of Ticonderoga in 1758, where he served the British in the French and Indian War.

Brant attended the Moors Indian Charity School, forerunner of Dartmouth College. He loved fine clothes, bore himself with dignity, and was a good businessman. Because of his connections to Sir William Johnson, the British representative to the Indians, Brant became involved with the efforts of the British to subdue the American colonies. After the war he settled in a village called Brantford in Canada, and lived until 1807.

On October 13, 1778, Brant and almost one hundred

Courtesy Minisink Valley Historical Society

Joseph Brant - Thayendenaga
(1743-1807)

Tories and Iroquois swept down through the Neversink Valley. They destroyed Fort Depuy and the provisions that were stored in it, as well as other storage areas, which left the settlers in a desperate situation. Several members of the pioneer families were killed. For the next winter many of the families lived together in the remaining forts including 113 in Fort Gumaer and 65 in Fort Dewitt.

An interesting account remains of that raid and comes from the Revolutionary War pension application of Martinus Decker. Lena Elmendorf attested in 1847, some 69 years after the event:

That she has a distinct recollection of border troubles of the Revolution - She recollects (sic) well that during those troubles she often had to stand and watch in fields while her father and brothers were at work to give the alarm when the Indians were seen lurking in the bushes and at several different times the whole family with others left their homes and crossed the Delaware into New York and New Jersey for safety.

That she was well acquainted with Martines Decker who lived on the New York side of the River and within two miles of where this deponent lived he was a Lieutenant in Capt Kortrights company and she has seen him out doing duty as such at several different times at the different rendvouses on the frontiers. She recollects that in the month of June 1778 the Indians made their appearance on the frontiers and the garrison on the Pennsylvania side of the River being very weak the Inhabitants fled across the River and went to Deckers fort where they remained for more than a week during that time Martines Decker was at the Fort doing duty as a Lieutenant at least one week. That this was the time when the Indians made a decent upon the people living in the valley of the Neversink and burned and destroyed several houses and barns killed Phillip Swartwout and his son and Lieutenant Stewart and old Levi Van Etten She further recollects that after the Indians left the Inhabitants who fled from Pennsylvania returned to their homes.

That in August or September the Indians were again discovered skulking about in the mountains and the garrison at Van Aukens Fort on the Pennsylvania side of the River being very weak consisting of only the old men and boys of the place Martines Decker crossed over from the York side of the River with twelve men and stationed himself there as guard and remained in the fort for two weeks he then acted as a Lieutenant this deponent was in the fort during the time and the reason why she recollects the time distinctly is that one day while he was there guarding at the fort a smoke was discovered in the mountain Lieutenant Decker with one of his men by the name of Nathan Van Auken started for the mountain to see what occasioned the smoke. They went into the woods but had not gone far before they were surprised by three Indians who lay in ambush and gave chase to them Van Auken being the activist out ran Decker and the Indians having nearly over taken him a brother of this deponents and a man by the name of Peter Van Auken each seized a gun ran out of the fort and fired at the Indians one of them they killed the others then made for the woods and escaped They two men then went out cut off the Indians head and brought it into the fort.

She is sure that Martines Decker served at the fort at this time at least two weeks as a Lieutenant. She always lived within a short distance of him until he died which was in 1802.

Another version of the 1778 raid comes from the affidavit of Peter Van Auken who in 1847 swore the following:

On this twenty eight day of July One thousand eight hundred and forty seven personally appeared before me Abraham J Cuddeback a Justice of the Peace in and for the County aforesaid Peter Van Auken a resident of Deerpark in the County of Orange and State of New York aged Eighty two years to me known as a man of truth and veracity and whose statements made are entitled to full credit and belief, who being first duly sworn according to law doth on his oath depose and say.

That the affidavit made by him sometime since in relation to the services of Lieutenant Martiness Decker in July 1778 is true That he knows and has a distinct recollection of Martiness Deckers being at the fort which surrounded the house of this deponents father on the Pennsylvania side of the Delaware River in July 1778 and acted as a Lieutenant for the term of two weeks and that during that time he went out one day with another person toward the mountain and was chased back toward the fort by three Indians.

The person with Decker out ran him and Decker halloed loudly for help when this deponent and one Middaugh each seized a musket and fired at the Indians and killed one of them the other two then retreated they thereby effected the escape of Lieutenant Decker. He this deponent cannot write and has always been in the habit of keeping time and accounts and business of different kinds in his memory.

That he recollects it was soon after they heard of the Battle of Monmouth he recollects that when they heard of that battle the militia held a Jubilee at the fort and it was but a few days after that when Lieutenant Decker was pursued by the Indians - He also recollects that a sister of his two years older than himself by the name of Katreen died while Lieutenant Decker and his men lay at the fort and he recollects that Decker superintended the affairs in relation to the funeral a sermon was preached by the Rev Mr Van Benschoeten and the Rev. Guetterman and Lieutenant

Decker walked together from the house to the grave which was but a few rods from the house in the corner of a field where she lay until after the enemy left the country when the corpse was taken up and conveyed across the Delaware River and buried in the Church yard in Deerpark He further says that he is not mistaken in his recollection of those facts He also recollects that it was the same year and about four weeks after the Indians killed the Swartwouts in Peenpack.

The second raid into the valley by Joseph Brant was equally disastrous. One local militiaman's widow who applied for a pension in later years wrote:

That on the nineteenth day of July 1779 long to be remembered by the people living in the valley of the Neversink the Indians again made their appearance on the frontiers and burned a number of houses and barns and destroyed much property.

The most dramatic day in the history of Fort Decker was July 20, 1779, when it was burned by Joseph Brant. Brant and approximately eighty of his men left Chemung, New York, and made their way to present-day Forestburgh, New York. Then, they swept down the Neversink Valley from present-day Cuddebackville. To relive the drama of that day so distant in the past, one can read the Revolutionary War pension application of Wilhelmus Westfall's wife Margaret. Although he had died in 1796, his wife was entitled to a pension for his service. In 1839, some sixty years after the event, she attested:

That in 1779 when the Indians attacked Minisink and burnt the houses and barns in that place her husbands house and barn and barrack with all their contents were destroyed they likewise set fire to the grist mill belonging to the family but did not accomplish the design the fire going out before it caught to the combustibles in the mill she further saith that she made her escape and saved her life by running and after travelling about five miles got into Vangorders fort. That in the month of April 1781 she again had to fly for her life and made her escape at the time that three of her husbands cousins were killed by the name of Joseph Jobs Lewis Westbrook and William Westbrook and she by the help of some friends she herself having just risen from a bed of sickness was enabled to cross the mountain to a

Courtesy Minisink Valley Historical Society

This nineteenth century rendering is entitled "The Escape of Captain Westfall's Wife." It also provides historians with another interpretation of what Fort Decker might have looked like.

Courtesy Minisink Valley Historical Society

There are two burned beams that are thought to be left from Brant's raid in 1779 in the basement of the building. The effort to remove the beams, when rebuilding was undertaken, would have been difficult and time-consuming. It was probably easier to leave them in place and build the new house around them.

place of safety

Brant's raiders followed the Horn Road in the Town of Deerpark, burning farms, destroying buildings, killing patriots and taking prisoners as they made their way to Machackemeck at the eastern edge of the Decker farm. "Lt. Martinus Decker's fort," as it is described in contemporary accounts, and his house, barn, sawmills and crops were all destroyed. Evidence of the raid remains in the house in the form of burned timbers in two corners of the basement. At least one account says that Brant's raiders pulled down one end of the abandoned building and set fire to the logs.

At the time, there were about eighteen families living in the "Lower Neighborhood" or the area now occupied by the city of Port Jervis. At least one account states a half-dozen families were living in Fort Decker at the time of the raid. Joseph Brant in his report on the raid also said that he had destroyed several other small stockaded forts. A report presented after the raid by Nathan Ker, the minister of the Presbyterian Church in Goshen, to George Clinton, the Governor of New York and the commander of its armed forces, reported that eleven houses were destroyed along with eleven barns and the Dutch church. Cattle, horses and plunder were taken by the raiders. Ker reported the loss of fifty to sixty men which had left fifteen or sixteen widows in his congregation in Goshen.

What defenses were put up against Brant is not clear. Again, the historical record is contradictory because Lt. Col. Albert Pawling, the commanding officer responsible for the frontier areas, reported he had twenty men stationed at Pienpack (Peenpack) in Godeffroy, New York at the time of the raid. Why they did not put up some defense of the valley, or at least figure into the accounts of the battle, is not known.

The Brant raid into the Neversink Valley was an effort to gain plunder and food for his people near Unadilla, and to spread terror to the frontier communities. In that goal he was successful. Brant was acquainted with the area because he had raided the valley the previous October. However,

Courtesy Minisink Valley Historical Society

in 1779 he made sure to destroy the property of one of the area's most ardent patriots, Martinus Decker, who was then believed to be living in the building.

After retreating up the Delaware Valley for the next two days, and being chased by the American militia, Brant was almost caught in a surprise attack but for the accidental discharge of a weapon by an American militia man. Militia units from Goshen, Warwick and Sussex met Brant at Minisink Ford, New York, and there the militiamen suffered a bloody defeat with at least forty-five Americans being killed. Militia leader Colonel John Hathorn described the dead as "so many brave men."

Many of the militiamen simply left the battle after it

Courtesy Minisink Valley Historical Society

began; some accounts suggest the number at almost one third. Governor Clinton would later write "there must have been some very bad management on this occasion, or the brave men who have fallen must have been shamefully deserted by their friends and I wish there was not too much reason to conclude the latter must have been the case."

Brant continued to move up the valley and back to his headquarters, while the families of those brave patriots mourned their losses. A party of two hundred and forty people traveled from Goshen to within several miles of the battle site to try and find the remains of those killed, but bad weather forced their return to Goshen. The battle at Minisink remains one of the most disastrous losses of the American Revolution proportional to participants. However, as indicated by Decker's continued service, the tragedies only stiffened his resolve to defeat the British.

Martinus Decker was probably not at the Fort that fateful day when his home was destroyed, his barn and crops burned, and his family traumatized. There was also a gristmill on the property. Today there are no nearby streams to provide a possible location, although they may have been diverted at a later time. He was forty-six years old, and his anger must have been great given that his life's work, and his family's heritage, had been destroyed.

At the time of Brant's second raid into the Delaware Valley in July, 1779, Wilhelmus Westfall and his family, according to tradition, were living in the stone house. It is also believed the families of Martinus Decker, Samuel Caskey, James Davis and Utley Westbrook were living there, perhaps six families in all. As many as 110 people were living in the Lower Neighborhood at the time.

The men of the Decker and Westfall families were apparently away scouting against an expected attack from the south near the Bushkill River in Pike County, Pennsylvania. Brant and his forces swept in from the north. These family members were not engaged with the militia units that met with defeat at the battle at Minisink Ford on July 22. They were apparently left to guard what was left of the settlement and deal with the destruction. As proof of that, the following comes from the widow of Martinus Decker who applied for a pension in 1839:

That on the 19th of July 1779 the Indians made a decent (sic) upon Minisink and destroyed the property of the Inhabittants by fire the alarm was given and the militia was called out and followed the Indians to a place called Beaver brook. Capt Kortrights company was called out and Lieutenant Decker was out in the said company as a Lieutenant from the time the alarm was given until he was discharged at least two weeks this service was under and part of the time under Col. Hathorn and Justin and the rest of the time was in the Fort called Decker Fort.

One of the main reasons the frontier region was so vulnerable to Brant's attack was that General George Washington had ordered Count Pulaski and his cavalry to leave the Minisink region earlier in the spring of 1779. About two-hundred and fifty men and horses had been stationed near Cole's Fort, where present-day East Main Street and Jersey Avenue meet. Men from local militia units were also transporting hundreds of prisoners of war, captured at the Battle of Stony Point, New York, just days before the Minisink raid occurred, to Easton, Pennsylvania. Three companies of Colonel Hathorn's Orange County militia unit had been ordered to undertake this task. John Sullivan's large force was gathering to the west and getting ready to begin laying waste to the Iroquois heartland in central New York.

In correspondence that followed among high-level officials, most were not sure where the attack was made in the Minisink and of the results. George Clinton described the actions of Brant's raiders as mischief; they were not sure what to do in light of the attacks. They believed the raid was a singular event and not a long drawn-out affair, and that the enemy would soon leave, as Joseph Brant did indeed do. Orders went out that a detachment be sent westward into the far reaches of Orange County, although an assessment was made later not to send them because the threat had diminished. It was not until October, 1779 that a sufficient defensive force was sent to the frontiers to defend the inhabitants.

There are many stories related to the Revolutionary War era and Brant's raid that have been passed down by descendants of the families that lived in the valley. No doubt the families living in both neighborhoods suffered greatly; the raiders made off with their best horses, plundered their homes, clothing, and destroyed the fruits of their labor.

At least one nineteenth century newspaper account said that Martinus Decker was involved in the battle, and shot Brant in the belt during an encounter near present-day Matamoras, Pennsylvania. Decker was said to have been hit in the ear by a shot from Brant. Brant is alleged to have said that he would torture Martinus Decker if he ever captured him. There is no evidence to confirm this story, particularly in Decker's service records, which might have recorded such a dramatic encounter.

Other accounts have Martinus Decker fighting at the battle but escaping, although that again is not cited in his pension records. It is hard to imagine that family members would not have remembered his participation in that tragic battle when they applied for his pension years later. One final story that has passed down through generations is that Decker watched his farm destroyed from a nearby mountain.

Another family story is of the rescue of Margaret Hayne by Wilhelmus Westfall from an Indian who attempted to kidnap her. Wilhelmus shot the Indian, and soon after married Margaret on June 17, 1778, in Wantage, New Jersey. The ceremony was conducted by Evi Adams, an acting Justice of the Peace for Sussex County, just prior to Brant's first raid on the Minisink settlements in October, 1778.

Another version of this story comes from a Kingston newspaper that said Margaret Hayne actually wanted to marry a man named DeWitt. DeWitt and Margaret Hayne were picking blackberries in an area between Fort Decker and the Delaware River. Wilhelmus Westfall, who was also in love with Margaret, and jealous of DeWitt, secretly followed them. He saw an Indian come upon Margaret Hayne and DeWitt. DeWitt fled, leaving Hayne behind. The Indian seized Margaret and began to take her away when Westfall overtook them, rescued Hayne, and brought her home along with the Indian's scalp. A wedding was said to have followed in 1780.

When Brant raided the settlements in 1779, DeWitt joined the raiders and helped them to remain undetected. When the raid upon Fort Decker began, Margaret Westfall fled, and DeWitt was allegedly killed at the battle at Minisink fighting for the British. Another Westfall tradition is that a "trusty Negro," who belonged to the Hayne family, buried valuable property belonging to the family and helped Margaret Westfall escape into the foothills of New Jersey.

Another sketchy account about the raid reports that in 1779, Andrew Dingman's son Isaac, aged 19, was fatally shot as he rode to his family's barn, and that the Indian who shot him hid in the family orchard. The next morning, the home of Henrick Decker was attacked and the families fled to Fort Decker. Two of Henrick Decker's sons, Henry and David, were killed, one being scalped.

There were several other military actions that occurred nearby. At the same time that Brant's raiders were making their way down the Delaware Valley, the Battle of Stony Point was taking place along the Hudson River. In this engagement the Americans recaptured the peninsula of land known as Stony Point under the leadership of General Anthony Wayne. This would be the last major battle in the northern colonies as the fighting shifted towards the south. A lasting peace, however, would not come to the valley until the declaration of peace in 1783, as George Washington's army was camped out at the New Windsor Cantonment, thirty-five miles east of Port Jervis.

Brant's raids were not the only incursions into the Neversink Valley during the war. In 1777 Indians slaughtered several families north of the junction of the Neversink and Delaware Rivers and moved down into Montague, although not much is known about that event.

THE REBUILDING OF FORT DECKER

After the buildings that were enclosed in the Fort Decker compound were destroyed during Brant's raid in 1779, it is generally agreed that the end walls of at least one building were all that was left standing. Between the raid and 1793 the historical record is not clear - was the house rebuilt and inhabited or left vacant? Nathan Ker, the Goshen minister, wrote on July 29, 1779: "The frontiers are in the utmost consternation and great numbers will no doubt soon leave their inhabitations unless properly guarded." As previously reported, it was not until October when the area was reinforced, giving residents reason not to leave their homes, or not to undertake any major rebuilding projects.

Archaeological work, completed in the last few years in the basement of Fort Decker, has not been conclusive, and only raised more questions as to what may have happened to the building complex. Revolutionary War-era artifacts were found near a former doorway. Additional test pits were dug in the center of the floor and after the first several inches of testing, no artifacts were found. No remnants of any fire damage were found at any soil level.

This would indicate the basement floor was cleared out after the fire and a clean layer of dirt left when the building was either repaired in 1779 or rebuilt in 1793. One might question whether the structure was the Fort or within the compound at all, but for the evidence of the burned beams at each end of the basement. A fire expert concluded after looking at the beams that the fire that burned them had been an intense one.

Many authors have written about the building's history but no one has completely reconciled what happened between 1779 and 1793. An 1887 newspaper article which provides the basis for much of the knowledge of the early history of the building seems to be accurate in most respects. It recounted that "A number of years after the burning of the old blockhouse - in 1793 - the debris was removed and the work of rebuilding commenced. The foundations were found to have received little or no injury and a portion of the walls remained intact."

Another history of the building written in 1902 states: "In rebuilding the structure in 1793, the foundations were found to have received little or no injury as a portion of the walls remained intact and form part of the present building." A 1903 article states that "The breach made by Brant's band was not repaired until 1793 when the walls were relaid with the stone that had originally formed it, and the log upper story was replaced by a stone one. With that exception, the building is the same as it was when first erected a century and a half ago."

The only author to suggest that something was actually done before 1793 is Jeanne Judson who, in a 1925 newspaper article, said that "After the cessation of hostilities between the

Colonies and England, Capt. and Mrs. Westfall sold the house, having first rebuilt it of stone from the foundation which were all the Indians had left standing." How Judson came to her conclusion and what her sources were are not known. In his seminal work, **History of Deerpark,** Peter Gumaer wrote that in the years following the American Revolution the state of the local economy was improved to such a degree that many of the residents began improvements both in their properties and possessions. That would seem to indicate that work may have been done before 1793, ten years after the peace was declared between Britain and its former colonies.

After a review of all these sources there are several possible scenarios. The first is that Lt. Martinus Decker's fort and surrounding buildings were simply abandoned in 1779. Perhaps there were other homes nearby not destroyed by Brant, that families moved into. *(Peter Decker and Frederick Hayne both had farms in Sussex County by this time.)* It seems unlikely the buildings would have been left vacant after the raid because of the valuable farm land surrounding them. Even if the families abandoned the house in the years of the Revolution (1776-1783), it seems that they would have refurbished the remains of the building for some purpose, if not a house. It seems unlikely they would have waited ten years after the Revolution to return.

Another scenario is that Wilhelmus Westfall was living in the house, or compound, and repaired it or one of the other buildings to live in after Brant's raid. One author believes that Captain Westfall left the building after the cessation of hostilities in 1783 and moved to Papakating Creek in Wantage Township, New Jersey. Another source says Decker returned to live at the stone house. For example, after the battle at Minisink Ford, correspondence between military officials referred to the blockhouse as "Lt. Martinus Decker's Fort."

A third possibility is that it did indeed sit vacant, a burned-out foundation, until 1793 when Martinus Decker undertook major renovations that are what we see today. These new improvements on the structure in 1793 came to be known as the rebuilding of Fort Decker.

All accounts agree that the foundation was intact when rebuilding was started and was used in that reconstruction. A close inspection of the joints in the stone of the house seems to indicate a line separating the old work and new work. One source says that only the foundation walls of the present-day building and a portion of "the upright walls," as they were called, are believed to remain from this original structure.

The author has concluded that the structure now known as Fort Decker was repaired after the raid and reinhabited. He also believes that the interior was essentially rebuilt from the first floor up to the second floor and attic in 1793. The stone exterior walls, particularly up to the place where the roof meets the gabled ends, are largely remnants of the pre-raid building, perhaps even the Haynes trading post. If the author is incorrect, one can presume the present building was, as other authors have suggested, built upon the foundation of what may have been one of several buildings that made up the "Martinus Decker settlement" prior to Brant's raid.

Additionally, what makes all of this unclear and perhaps unknowable, is that it still is not known how or when the stone house and adjoining lands came into the possession of Martinus

Decker. Some accounts suggest that Westfall sold the property to Decker. One plausible explanation is that both the Westfall and Decker families were living in the building(s) at the same time or perhaps had joint ownership. With Catherine Decker Hayne, a daughter of Peter Decker, being married to Frederick Hayne, and Margaret Hayne, a daughter of Frederick, being married to Wilhelmus Westfall, this seems possible.

The reconstructed Fort Decker with its center hall is typical of the Georgian and Dutch Colonial architectural styles popular in the Delaware and Hudson river valleys in the late 1700s. It was built on a north-south line with its front facing east to catch the sun and is also a short distance from a waterway, the Delaware River. The house is one-and-a-half stories, typical for the period. Decker chose a building style which his family was familiar with; he used a masonry construction technique that dated back to his ancestors, which reflects the rocky landscape of the area, and the need for protection from attack. Stone houses dotted the region along the Old Mine Road which ran from Kingston to the Delaware Water Gap in New Jersey. Many of the stone houses in the region have a similar design.

Typically, the cellar was excavated first and then irregular fieldstones or rubble stones, found during the excavation of the cellar and in the nearby fields, were given a "face" or flat surface which formed the exterior wall of the building. Large stones were interlocked with smaller stones which were held together by gravity and very little mortar.

As the eighteenth century ended, at the time Martinus Decker was rebuilding his house, the tooling of stone increased. Usually, the front side of a house was its best side, with the most tooled stone. This tooling technique is very much in evidence at Fort Decker. Most of the rubble stone used was river-bottom material, although there is an occasional piece of stone with a different color and texture. On the north side of the building is at least one piece of pink Shawangunk quartz and a number of rocks that contain fossils. One wonders what Martinus Decker and the people of his generation thought of the fossils imprinted in the stone. Would they have believed them to be about four thousand years old - the result of the great flood of Noah's time?

Crevices were filled with an improvised mortar that consisted mainly of river-bottom mud mixed with lime. Samples of

Courtesy Minisink Valley Historical Society

While Fort Decker's exterior walls are stone, this illustration demonstrates how the roof, floors, chimney and interior walls were constructed.

There is a noticeable difference in the stonework on the front side of the building. Its appearance is more finished and horizontal, and less random than the sides and the back of the building.

this white mortar can still be seen on the building's exterior. The wood for the beams, paneling, doors and windows were probably taken from the property. The interior support walls were given an initial layer of horsehair, grass and mud laid on lath. A finish coat of lime plaster was put over the interior walls as well as the exterior walls, where the plaster was laid directly on the stone, creating a somewhat uneven finished surface.

To give some perspective of how widespread the use of stone was, some two hundred stone houses still stand in present-day Ulster County, New York. It is thought as many were torn down early in the twentieth century. There were probably several other stone houses within present-day Port Jervis, and probably ten or more in the town of Deerpark, several of which still

Visitors often confuse the walls in the basement that support the hearth with a closed fireplace. However, these massive structures were used to support both the hearth and the weight of the enormous fireplaces.

stand. A 1798 census shows about twenty-five percent of the homes in the area were made of stone.

    Stone houses were usually constructed under the supervision of a housewright, who hired a mason and several other helpers to hew and plane logs, create doors and windows, and plaster the walls. It usually took about four to six months to build a stone house.

    During the 1793 reconstruction, Martinus Decker placed a large smooth datestone, which was made from bluestone, in the northern gable of the building . It is inscribed with his initials (MD), his second wife's initials (MD) and "CD mason." Some have suggested that the CD represents his sister Catherine's initials. What is not clear then is what the word "mason" would signify. Another more likely explanation is that "CD mason" is actually the housewright or mason's initials. Masons and carpenters were often hired to construct stone houses, and Coykendall Decker may have been the builder, as his initials match those of a man listed in the 1798 Federal census, whose occupation is shown as a stone mason.

The front window casings are original (at least to 1793) as are the second-floor window casings. None of the sashes is original, and several may date from the early twentieth century. Late nineteenth century photographs show the building's windows with a twelve-over-six configuration, which may be the

Courtesy Richard Tarbell

The datestone from 1793 remains in place in the northern gable.

Courtesy Peter Osborne

Evidence of fine workmanship remains throughout the building. To construct window casings, pegs were used to join the corners. In addition, a beading on the corner of the woodwork, both interior and exterior, is still visible.

original (1793). The window sashes were then altered in the early twentieth century, the front window panes being twelve-over-eight and the gable side window panes on the first floor being nine-over-six. The shutters that were on the building after 1793 were probably paneled like the current ones; the louvered shutters shown in late nineteenth-century drawings were probably added after the Deckers sold the property. Shutter pin holes have only been found on the windows in the front of the building.

The building has only been painted five or six times since its reconstruction. The initial coat was white, a color often used by the Anglo-Dutch. The second color was black. Since 1980 the building has been painted three times, using a cream color that was common in Orange County along with a dark green for the shutters and porch.

Planes were used to finish the wood and also to create a bead, or "reed" on the exposed ceiling beams, the window casings, and the fascia boards on the gabled ends of the building. Iron hinges for doors, nails and brackets were made by local blacksmiths. The trim on the gable ends, the window casings, first floor support beams which were hand-cut, beams, pegs and floorboards were all created in the 1793 reconstruction. A roof of hand-split wooden shakes was installed.

Two basement doors also existed; both have since been filled in. The first, on the southern side of the building, was filled in during the last quarter of the nineteenth century. This opening may have actually existed in the pre-reconstructed building. The second entrance, on the northern end, was filled in after 1970.

A 1915 newspaper article described a well located in

Courtesy Walpack Historical Society

It is not known what the original fireplace looked like in the parlor room of Fort Decker. This sketch of the keeping room at the Van Campen Inn in Walpack, New Jersey, is probably similar to what the original woodwork looked like.

front of the building which may have dated from the Decker period and can be traced back at least to the 1840s. There has been speculation there was a cistern in the basement of the building that would have been used in the event of a water shortage when the building was under attack. However, recent archaeological activity did not find the remains of any such feature in the basement.

The interiors of rural Anglo-Dutch houses of the period follow similar patterns. There is a formal or parlor room, as there is in the southern first-floor room of this building, and a common room, where cooking was done, as there is in the northern part of the first floor of this building. Beds were placed in all rooms, and in many Dutch houses there were no separate bedrooms. If there were additional rooms, they were used by the hired hands, slaves or servants.

Courtesy Peter Osborne

One of the few pieces left from the Decker family's occupancy of the stone house is the corner cupboard constructed at the time the house was rebuilt. Paint samples were taken from the cupboard and match colors throughout the house. It is not known who built the cupboard. HL hinges which can be seen on the doors are of English origin.

Courtesy Peter Osborne

The original pegs on which families hung their clothing remain in the central hall.

Portions of the building's first floor interior features remain intact from 1793, and include fireplaces as well as a fireplace crane, part of the cooking oven and the handsome corner cupboard. A central hall with entrances into both rooms and doors that opened to the exterior at either end were a typical feature. The enclosed staircase to the second floor proved to be an important feature, as it kept heat confined to the first floor.

The large exposed floor beams, evenly placed and finished with a handsome beading, are typical of Dutch houses. In the early decades of the nineteenth century they were covered over with a plaster on lathe ceiling. The shadows of the lathing is still visible. The original walls were plastered with a lime and sand mixture and then whitewashed with a lime, salt and water mixture.

Hand-carved pegs for hanging clothes remain in the first-floor hall. Both stairwells date from this time, including the paneling on the staircase leading to the second floor. The late Roy Vail, a well-known architectural historian living in Orange County, also believed the back door was original to the building. The author, however, questions this conclusion because the hinge plates do not line up with the original hardware.

Most of the second floor's 1793 features remain intact,

including the vertical paneling, batten doors, hardware and plaster. An interesting feature in the house is that the second floor walls are not plastered but covered with planed boards, numbered individually with Roman numerals and cut by a gouge. This indicates that they may have been brought from a carpenter's shop, numbered at a sawmill to indicate board feet or perhaps even brought from another building.

Vail believed the ceiling boards dated from a later time, and that the second floor did not originally have any fireplaces. There is some early nineteenth century graffiti in the bedroom with the fireplace, perhaps left over from the time the building was a canal hotel in the early nineteenth century. The front and back entrances probably had Dutch doors, constructed in two separate pieces to allow the top to remain open while the bottom was kept closed, preventing livestock from coming into the house. The casing surrounding the front door was probably closed in the mid-nineteenth century when the porch was added.

As one looks at the building's exterior, the proportion of all of the features is handsome and nicely done. There is something simple and yet elegant about the stone house from afar. As Harrison Meeske said in his landmark study **The Hudson Valley Dutch and Their Houses,**

Courtesy Peter Osborne

Numbered boards line the walls and floor boards of the second floor and cellarway.

"style and fashion were not a concern." Neil Larsen, a regional preservation expert, has observed that the builders of houses like Fort Decker have "a certain honesty and integrity to the craftsmanship, a directness. It relates to the kind of restrained, plain aesthetic the settlers worked with. One can sense it was really more the integrity of craftsmanship than the application or embellishment of ornament that determined the aesthetic. That is something we tend to attribute to the people who built these houses - directness, restraint and seriousness." And that, perhaps, is also a good description of Martinus Decker as well.

THE DECKER FARM

It is not known how the property that encompassed the Decker farm was acquired by Martinus Decker. Perhaps Hayne built his trading post on Peter Decker's land, or just operated the trading post that was owned by the Deckers. As with Frederick Hayne, it is also not known if the Westfalls owned the land that Fort Decker is located on or if they rented or lived in one of the Decker houses. Unfortunately no deeds have been found relative to the property prior to 1798, so the abstract of title prior to 1798 cannot be determined. Perhaps it is unknowable at this late date.

The Decker family's farms were large operations that began sometime in the early 1700s and continued until the early 1800s when Martinus Decker's son, Richard, finally sold the property. The earliest land transaction in which Martinus Decker is mentioned is found in the Orange County, New York land records, and is dated 1798. These records are held in the Orange County Government Center in Goshen. Additional research was conducted in Kingston, New York, (Ulster County) and Newton, New Jersey (Sussex County); no land records with

Martinus Decker's name could be found.

Additional records might have existed in Kingston because the western part of Orange County bordered Ulster County and in some cases landowners actually thought they were in Ulster County. The records were searched in Newton because the Decker properties were clearly below the Jersey Claim Line of 1719 according to the proprietors of East and West Jersey.

It has been suggested, although no citation is offered, that Frederick and Margaret Hayne passed the title of the building to Martinus Decker. Charles Stickney wrote that William Tiestsort (Titsworth), believed to be the first European to settle in the area, sold the land given to him by the local Indians, to John Decker and his cousin, "young Jan" in 1713. Because of the confusion surrounding the Decker family's genealogy, it is not clear who this Jan was. Another author thought Jan Decker (Peter Decker's father and Martinus Decker's grandfather) owned most of what is now Port Jervis. This provides us with the most likely scenario given that the Deckers were in the valley more than twenty years before Frederick Hayne.

One may wonder why the deeds were recorded in 1798 and not earlier; there are two plausible explanations. The first is that Martinus was beginning to get ready to transfer his property to his sons. This may have been because of health reasons or simply that he was almost sixty-five years old, and wanted to have a smooth transition in place for his family.

Another consideration may have been acts of state legislation that were working their way through the system. In 1788 the Orange County boundary line was extended to include a small part of present-day Deerpark and the entire city of Port Jervis. In that year the Town of Minisink, which did include the area currently occupied by the city, was incorporated.

In 1798 a new Orange-Ulster county boundary line was drawn; Port Jervis was still included in Minisink. This would not change until 1825 when Port Jervis, and parts of the current Town of Deerpark, were taken from the Town of Minisink and included in a newly-enlarged Town of Deerpark. As the eighteenth century ended, the political and legal boundaries in the region were more clearly settled than at any time since the Deckers had arrived in the Minisink.

The Decker family's combined land holdings extended across Orange and Sullivan counties, and into the present-day

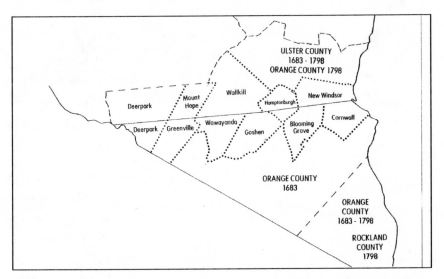

Courtesy Minisink Valley Historical Society

The original boundaries of Orange County were quite different prior to 1798. Orange included the present-day Rockland County as well as part of Ulster County.

Sussex Borough and Wantage Township in Sussex County, New Jersey. Members of the Hayne, Westfall and Decker families, over time, moved to the Papakating Valley in Sussex County, and continued to live in close proximity to each other.

The Deckers owned property at Halfway Brook, near present-day Barryville, New York, where Peter Decker built a sawmill. It is worth noting that Peter Decker purchased this property in 1761, which is recorded in the **Abstract of Sussex County Deeds** compiled by James McCoy. This is of particular interest because if the abstract is correct, it is very near to where Brant and his raiders camped during their raid in 1779. Could Brant have known that the land they were camped on, or near, was that of Peter and Martinus Decker? When Peter Decker died, he left the property to his sons Martinus and Joseph.

The Martinus Decker farm was a large one, at least two hundred acres, bounded by the Delaware River to the west, to the edge of the Appalachian plateau to the north and following the river-bottom lands to approximately where Pike Street is today. Having been one of the earliest families to stake land claims here, they were among the largest landowners. Most of the river-bottom area of Port Jervis was owned by the Deckers or allied families.

The family, based on research in various wills and documents, apparently held their possessions through joint ownership arrangements, probably a common practice at the time. A tract of seven hundred acres along the Neversink River was owned jointly by Martinus and Peter Decker until 1774. Peter Decker's 1773 will, probated in 1774, indicates he and his son Matthias *(probably Martinus, due to a misreading of the handwriting)*

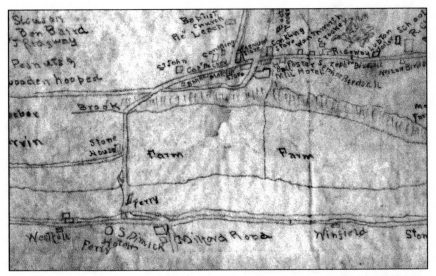

Courtesy Minisink Valley Historical Society

The actual dimensions of the Decker farm are not known, although the author believes it is where the area is marked "farm." Fort Decker is noted as the stone house on the left side.

owned a large farm bordering on the Machackemek (Neversink) River. The deed says it was located at Waghmackemeck (Mahackamack) and believed to be in present-day Port Jervis. Another deed, dated June 30, 1798, transferred land bordering the Delaware, and may have been for the farm adjacent to Fort Decker on the northwestern side, or the main farm itself. The deed is from Martinus Decker and his wife, Mary, to Samuel Caskey, Richard Decker and John Decker.

Property assessments and census records also shed some clues on the Deckers' landholdings and property. An assessment roll in 1775 shows two Martinus Deckers, one a Sr. and one a Jr., with the senior holding six pounds and seventeen shillings worth of property, while the junior held seven shillings. The 1790

Federal Census, in which Martinus Decker and his family are listed, indicates they did not own slaves. However, several other Decker families did, as well as many of the other large landowners. Martinus' son, Peter, did have another person living in his house who may have been an apprentice.

The population of the entire town of Minisink *(which then included present-day Port Jervis and a portion of the towns of Deerpark and Minisink)* was 2,215. There were 370 heads of families and only 51 slaves. Goshen, which had a slightly larger population, had 212 slaves.

In 1798, Congress passed a law that called for a uniform valuation of lands, dwelling houses and slaves within the United States, with the ultimate purpose of taxing all of its citizens more fairly. This was the first time this kind of national property assessment was ever proposed and also the last. The information culled from that census has proven to have great historical value. The 1798 assessment records provide researchers with valuable insights.

In the enumeration district that included a part of Deerpark, there were forty-nine homes. The dimensions of the typical house were about thirty feet long, twenty-five feet wide, one story high and contained five small windows. One quarter of the homes were built of stone, and about half of the houses in the town were considered to be in a "middling" condition. Thirteen of the houses were considered old and none was considered new. Out of the forty-nine homes, there were only two homes that were two stories. The average size of all those homes, the larger homes excepted, was seven hundred and fifty square feet.

These records also provide additional insights and accurate descriptions of the Decker family's assets, which were then located in the Town of Minisink. There is a contemporary description of Martinus Decker's house and farm in the federal property assessment which states that "Martinus Decker owned a stone house that was one story high, and measured twenty-four by thirty-nine feet. There were two windows, 2½ x 4 feet in size, two windows 2 x 4 feet in size and three windows 1½ x 2 feet in size. The property was located next to the property of Samuel Caskey, and assessed on one acre of land, considered in good condition and assessed by the principal assessor at $390 .

Courtesy Peter Osborne

There was probably at least one barn on the property to store hay and to house livestock. Its location has not been determined, although it has been speculated that the house across the street from Fort Decker, pictured here, may enclose what was the original barn.

. . The house was located on a farm, and the barn was thirty by twenty-two feet and two hundred and twenty acres of property assessed by the principal assessor at $1,625. This made the total value of the house and farm - $2,015."

This special assessment listed the principal house, if it was valued at over one hundred dollars and included more than one acre of land, as a separate item. So in the case of Martinus Decker's stone house, it is listed separately, adjoining Samuel Caskey, where the old "Caskey line" was located. This property line division is currently the boundary line that divides the Minisink Valley Historical Society's property from the Port Jervis Fire Department's property and forms the basis for property lines of more than twelve other properties up to the railroad right-of-way, and the base of Mount William.

Martinus' son Richard had forty-five acres and a house worth $20 adjoining his father's land, and Samuel Caskey had a house valued at $15 with thirty-five acres adjoining Martinus', presumably on the west side of the Caskey line. Martinus Decker's name is also found in the 1798 Town of Minisink's Cattle Brand Book and Town Tax Book along with that of two of his sons.

Martinus Decker turned over the remaining tracts of land, which at that time probably included much of lower West End and the former Erie railroad yards, to his son Richard in 1801. Upon his death in 1802 Martinus Decker's will was probated, and its provisions left his wife the furniture, cows, sheep, horses, her hunting saddle, and any debts that were owed to him. A portion of the land that he still owned, which amounted to about 165 acres, was divided between his sons. The executors of

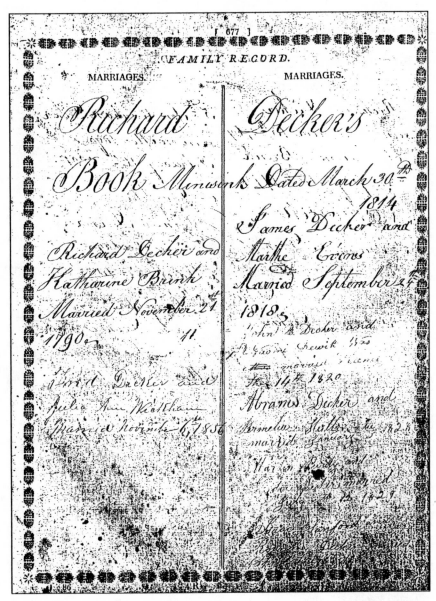

A page from the Richard Decker family Bible. It is one of the few artifacts associated with the family that has come back to the Society.

his will were his wife and son-in-law Samuel Caskey.

His family continued to live in the area. Richard Decker (1767-1851) continued the ownership of the stone house property. He was married on November 21, 1790, to Katherine Brink (1774-?), and by this marriage there were eight children. One of the few remaining family heirlooms that is now in the possession of the Society, the Richard Decker family Bible, is on display in the stone house. Decker was active in Town of Minisink affairs, and was appointed a constable at the town's second meeting in 1790.

Son John (1765-1843) remained in the area, perhaps moving to Sussex County, New Jersey. Another son of Martinus, Martin (1770-1829?), stayed in the area not far from the former Decker farm. His name appears in a school district listing in 1813, along with his brothers-in-law, the Caskeys. Richard Decker sold the stone house and surrounding lands to John Kent in 1815. The deed states that Richard Decker was still living in the stone house at the time of sale, and that Samuel Stickney lived in a portion of the house, probably a clapboard section at the rear, from which he operated a grocery store. At least one account states that Kent came to own the property because of an exchange of property somewhere else, and that he and his brother-in-law, William K. Stone, lived in the house.

Richard Decker and his family moved to the Midwest and other Deckers went to New Jersey and Pennsylvania, reflecting a national trend of people moving westward in search of new land and horizons when the fertility of the valley's soil decreased. With the departure of Richard Decker, the family's connection to the building ended.

THE ST. JOHN HOTEL

During the late 1820s the Delaware and Hudson Canal Company, the first American corporation capitalized at one million dollars, began to construct an extensive transportation network that extended from Carbondale, Pennsylvania, to Kingston, New York. The whole system was about 170 miles long, and included a 108-mile-long canal and sixty-mile-long gravity railroad. The system shipped anthracite coal from the mountains west of Honesdale, Pennsylvania, to Kingston, New York. It was opened in 1828.

A portion of the canal passed through the Decker property, paralleling the present-day railroad line at the base of Mount William. It was during this time that the building and farm came into the possession of Stephen St. John (1788-1870), who would ultimately become one of the richest men in Port Jervis. His land dealings had a significant impact on the development of the City, both as a canal center and later as a railroad center.

Stephen St. John was born November 16, 1788, in Norwalk, Connecticut, and when he was fourteen years old he went to New York City to make a living. He apprenticed as a shoemaker and stayed in the business for several years, becoming a successful merchant. He came to Port Jervis, and started a small store in a building owned by Mrs. Parmel Mondon, at the corner of Main Street and Kingston Avenue. He operated the business until 1808 when he tried a new line of work, entering into a partnership with a Mr. Holly. They purchased a tannery at a location somewhere between Mount Hope and Middletown. During this time St. John built up a large business and enjoyed widespread recognition. His business career was interrupted by the War of 1812, when he served with a unit until 1815.

At the conclusion of the war, the area that includes present-day Port Jervis and the surrounding Town of Deerpark was occupied mainly by descendants of the early Dutch settlers. The most heavily settled area was near Carpenter's Point, present-day Tri-States. It was during this time, in 1819, that John Kent sold the Decker house and farm to Benjamin Dodge and Stephen St. John for $5,000. It was also during this period that St. John entered into a partnership with Benjamin Dodge, and opened another store. Soon they moved their business to Mount Hope. Benjamin Dodge was active in the civic affairs of Mount Hope, including the Masonic Lodge; he was also a good businessman. He served as an inspector of schools, and was on the board of directors of the Mount Hope and Lumberland Turnpike, which began near Dodge's store at the junction with the Minisink and Montgomery Turnpike.

St. John came home every Saturday, some twelve miles, to spend Sunday with his family, and then returned to Mount Hope on Monday. In October, 1816, he married Abigail Horton (1792-

1870) of Mount Hope, and they remained together until her death. They moved to the stone house before 1820 because all of their children were born there including: Charles (1819-1891), Amira (1826-1909), Philenda (1827-1901), Amelia (1829-1894), and Horace (1833-1860).

All three daughters married men who became prominent in the community's affairs. Amira married Samuel W. Mills, who was a minister in the Reformed Church and the first President of the Minisink Valley Historical Society. He was also the author of some of the early newspaper articles that describe the history of the stone house. Philenda married George Malven, who was an owner of the Malven and Gordon Stove Works compa-

Courtesy Minisink Valley Historical Society

The D & H Canal was one of the great transportation corporations of the nineteenth century. It carried anthracite coal from the mines of northeastern Pennsylvania to New York City and New England markets. This barge, typical of those used, is getting ready to cross the Delaware Aqueduct at Minisink Ford, New York.

ny. Amelia married Francis Marvin, a distinguished attorney. The sons were prominent businessmen in Port Jervis. The St. John's continued to operate the Decker land as an active farm until the property began to be subdivided and sold off.

In 1826, as the Delaware and Hudson Canal was being built, canal officials Maurice Wurts, Philip Hone and John B. Jervis negotiated for a right-of-way across the St. John property. St. John then sold the company some of his land and was also employed as its toll collector in Port Jervis, where there was a large canal basin on the site of the present-day Port Jervis Bowl. As one of the company's most important employees on this section of the canal, St. John was a trusted advisor to its managers and engineers, and was in its service until 1870. He was a major landholder in Sullivan County, where he owned several sawmills.

Courtesy Minisink Valley Historical Society

John. B. Jervis

c. 1830

St. John also took on another partner, Dr. John Conkling. St. John continued as an active manager in his businesses until 1839, when he retired and turned control over to his son, Charles.

Stephen St. John, an astute businessman, also used his home, known as the "St. John Canal Hotel," to accommodate canal laborers and engineers during the construction of the canal. John B. Jervis, for whom the city is named,

Courtesy Minisink Valley Historical Society

Russel F. Lord

c. 1855

stayed at the stone house regularly while he served as Chief Engineer for the canal company. Russel F. Lord, Jervis' successor, also stayed there on occasion during the canal's construction, and after it was completed. Lord would serve as Chief Engineer until 1863. Some accounts, including the historic marker in front of Fort Decker, say Jervis stayed there for the entire time he was chief engineer. However, Jervis, in his autobiography, clearly states that he stayed in Mamakating for most of the time that he oversaw the canal's construction. Lord, Jervis and St. John carried on a friendship that lasted many years.

The canal had a profound impact on communities along its length. Area residents benefited by the arrival of the waterway in a number of ways: they were employed to build and maintain the project, worked in boatyards, operated boats, were able to purchase finished goods from the metropolitan area, and shipped local goods to larger markets. The canal opened the interior of a region that had been lightly populated and where Dutch had been spoken in church services until the 1790s.

It was during the 1820-1835 period that much of the interior woodwork that still remains in the stone house was installed on the first floor. The house was remodeled in the

Courtesy Minisink Valley Historical Society

Not only did Stephen St. John's house serve as a hotel for canal company employees, but he also served as the toll collector for the Port Jervis section of the canal. The building pictured here on the right was his office, and was located at the corner of Canal and West Main Streets.

Federal style, with plaster ceilings, mantelpieces, new doorways in the hall and a hallway being added. The cupboard in the first floor kitchen was moved and a window installed in the stone wall behind where it had stood. The beehive oven was probably removed at this time, and a coal stove installed. The kitchen may have also been divided into several rooms.

Because of the substantial walls, stone houses were difficult to expand with similar kinds of material, so in the early 1800s a large wood frame addition was constructed at the rear of Fort Decker to provide extra space, and probably used in con-

Courtesy Richard Tarbell

The St. John Canal Hotel sign provides the oldest known image of Fort Decker. It shows no front porch, an eight-panel front door, an addition that was actually on the backside and an orchard. There were no windows at the end of the building and various kinds of fencing can be seen along the canal.

junction with the hotel operation. This addition survived at least until the 1890s, and a portion of the foundation line can still be seen in the ground now occupied by the brick border of the herb garden. The rest of the foundation can be seen when the grass dries out during the dry summer months.

The paneled fireplace in the former parlor room was altered, and the current mantle was installed along with the brick insert. The paneling was probably removed, and a closet was eliminated to construct a new window on the south end of the building. Until the renovation work was begun in the 1970s, the building's first floor interior appearance dated from about 1830, with its exterior retaining its 1793 appearance. This process was

Courtesy Peter Osborne

The St. John family left Fort Decker and built this house on West Main Street. The house no longer stands.

typical of the progression of improvements done to older homes as owners tried to keep pace with fashion, different architectural styles, changing technology and economics. It may have been during this time that the parlor room was divided into two rooms.

In 1830 there were only four buildings in the area that would be called Germantown in the late nineteenth century, and is now called West End. Two of the homes were owned by Caskeys, and the third by Simon Westfall. Stephen and Abigal St. John lived in the stone house, the fourth, until 1836 when they moved to a newly-built home at the base of Mount William on present-day West Main Street. That building was demolished in 1943. A district school stood on the hill above Fort Decker, near where the present-day railroad bridge enters West End.

St. John made another astute business decision in 1846 when proposals for the construction of the Erie Railroad were being considered. He subdivided the remaining acres of the large farm and sold sixty acres of land, at $100 per acre, to the Erie Railroad Company, a sum many considered to be exceedingly large at the time. This land allowed the development of rail yards and a division center. It is now the site of buildings owned by Kolmar Laboratories (2006), the former K-Mart plaza and the turntable/roundhouse properties, owned by the City of Port Jervis (2006). Because of wise investments and timely sales of his property, St. John became a wealthy man. When he died in 1870 his estate was worth $269,431, including four hundred shares in the Delaware and Hudson Canal Company, valued at $49,000.

Stephen St. John was active in the community, belonging

Courtesy Peter Osborne

The final resting place of Abigal and Stephen St. John.

to and supporting the Deerpark Reformed Church, and a member of the Port Jervis Lodge of Masons. He also served as a school commissioner, and the school district was, in part, defined by his farm's boundaries. He served on the first Board of Directors of the Bank of Port Jervis in 1853, but he was never involved in local politics. St. John was a plain, temperate, frugal man, and a kind parent, according to his obituary; he was held in kind remembrance after he died.

Abigail St John died in the spring of 1870, and was described at the time of her death as a kindhearted and charitable person. Stephen St. John died several months later in September. After a funeral service attended by many of his fellow citizens at the Deerpark Reformed Church, he was buried in an adjacent graveyard that bore his name, the St. John's Burying Ground. Abigail had also been buried there in the family's vault. The graveyard was located on the ground now occupied by the playground at the corners of Sullivan Avenue and East Main Street.

In 1884 an act of the State Legislature was passed that allowed the abandonment of the burying ground to allow the construction of a schoolhouse. Also known as the "Old Churchyard Burial Ground," the cemetery was closed in the spring of 1885, and the remains, including those of the St. John family, were removed to other local cemeteries. His family purchased a large plot in Laurel Grove Cemetery overlooking the bend in the Delaware River and his remains were reinterred there.

Courtesy Minisink Valley Historical Society

This late nineteenth century line drawing of Fort Decker shows the house as it would have appeared in Stephen St. John's lifetime. A wooden frame addition extended beyond the back of the building and was sided with clapboard. The windows appear to still have the original sashes along with louvered shutters. A wooden picket fence, long gone, surrounded the front of the property.

In a late nineteenth century newspaper article recalling the history of Fort Decker, the stone house was described as the "old mansion," something that would have brought a smile to the face of Stephen St. John, and most certainly to the Deckers and Westfalls who lived there before him.

A grandson of Stephen St. John, Charles (1849-1914), and son of Charles (1819-1891)) was also engaged in the hotel business. Charles St. John owned and operated the High Point Inn on High Point Mountain in Wantage, New Jersey, within site of the stone house, from 1890-1907. Overlooking Lake Marcia, it was three hundred feet long, thirty-two feet wide, two stories high and had a magnificent view of the surrounding region. The Adirondack-styled structure could accommodate up to two hundred guests and had sixty-six double rooms.

The grandson also owned two other resorts, *The Piney Woods Inn* and *Oak Hall*, both located in Southern Pines, North Carolina. In 1911 he purchased another resort, *The Gates*, in Hendersonville, North Carolina, and changed its name to *The Saint John*. One can imagine that he was following in his grandfather's footsteps, although on a much grander scale. In his grandfather's day a number of prominent men were probably squeezed into one of the small rooms on the second floor of the stone house in conditions that could only be described as fairly primitive by the grandson's standards. At the High Point Inn there were, according to advertisements, "Comfortable beds, a first class table, a summer resort with all the conveniences of city life." Entertaining guests ran in the family.

THE DECKER STONE HOUSE IN
THE NINETEENTH CENTURY

After the canal hotel closed in the 1830s, the original Decker farm property continued to be subdivided into smaller lots. And, for the next one hundred and twenty-five years the Decker stone house served as a private residence. The building that had witnessed so many important events faded into the background of the city's growing and urbanized landscape.

The house was rented out to a number of families, at least two of whom are known: the Youman family in the 1830s and the Mackin family during the 1850s and 1860s. Charles Mattice, a long-time Erie Railroad employee, was born in the house on March 12, 1865. An interesting citation can be found in the 1880 census when it lists sixteen people living at Fort Decker: members of the John Cannon family (six) and the Richard Tracy family (ten). However, with few records available until the 1880s, the history of the building between 1830 and 1890 again remains shrouded in mystery.

In the last years of his life, Stephen St. John began subdividing and selling his remaining landholdings in the Germantown section of Port Jervis. Upon his death in 1870, the

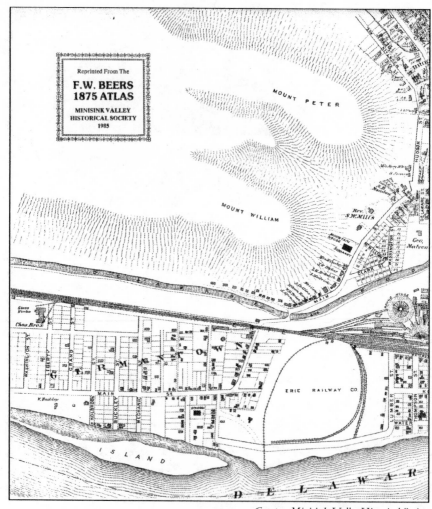

Courtesy Minisink Valley Historical Society

Upon the death of Stephen St. John in 1870, executors of his estate continued to subdivide his large land holdings in the Germantown section of
Port Jervis. It is now known as West End. This allowed for the development of the Erie Railroad's engine facilities and yards. Fort Decker is located where Main Street turns northeast, directly in line with the notation
"Erie Railway Co."

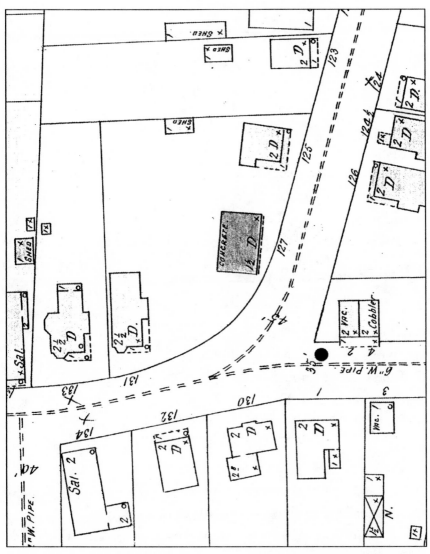

Courtesy Minisink Valley Historical Society

The property containing the stone house and the current addresses at 125, 127, 131 and 133 West Main Street are shown on this turn-of-the-century fire insurance map. Fort Decker is described as a concrete building. The properties now make up the Fort Decker Compound.

executors of his estate continued this process so that by 1875 only the lots for 125, 127, 131 and 133 West Main Street remained of what had been the large Decker farm.

The properties containing the stone house (127) and the neighboring addresses at 125, 131 and 133 West Main Street were sold to a recent Irish immigrant named John Cannon, Sr. by Stephen St. John in 1865. The purchase price was $2,400, and the contract was structured so that Cannon paid $600 upon delivery of the contract, and then a mortgage was taken to be repaid in three years. This contract must have been extended at least once because a deed transferring the property to Cannon is dated 1872, when the executors of St. John's estate finally signed off.

Like the Hayne, Westfall and Decker genealogies, the Cannon family genealogy is worth reciting because the family also had a long association with the building. In fact it is believed that the Cannon family owned the stone house property longer than the Deckers did. The first generation begins with John Cannon, Sr. (1804-1884?) and his wife, Rose Gray (1805-1886?). From passenger-list records it is known that John and Rose Cannon arrived in America from Ireland on March 28, 1864. They had embarked in Liverpool, England on the ship named the "Escort" and passed through New York City.

John and Rose purchased Fort Decker, and the other nearby lots, as previously noted, and built a house at 125 West Main Street in 1870. It is believed that John Cannon, Sr. lived at Fort Decker from 1865-1870 and then lived at 125 West Main Street from 1870 until his death about 1884. Of Rose, we know almost nothing except that she was still alive in 1886(?) and liv-

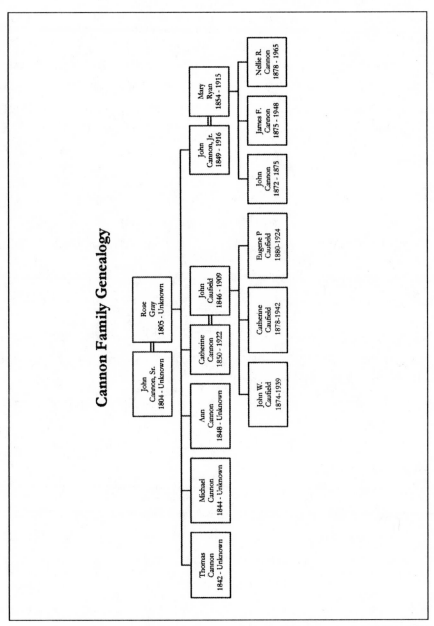

Courtesy Nancy Conod and Nancy Vocci

The John Cannon Sr. family genealogy

ing several blocks away at 173 West Main Street with her daughter Catherine Caufield. It is not known when either John or Rose Cannon died. It is also not known exactly where they are buried although it is believed they may be buried with their daughter Catherine in unmarked graves at St. Mary's Cemetery in Port Jervis.

By their marriage there were five children, all of whom were born in Ireland: Thomas Cannon (1842-?), Michael Cannon (1844-?), Ann Cannon (1848-), John Cannon, Jr. (1849-1916) and Catherine Cannon (1850-1922). The child we know the most about is John, Jr. who married Mary Ryan (1854-1915) on February 16, 1877. John, Jr. came to America from Ireland with his parents, and he immediately began work with the Erie Railroad Company. In the 1874 City Directory he was listed as a laborer, in 1880 as a fireman and by 1887 he was an engineer. He retired in 1915 as a firemen on the railroad. He and his wife attended Sacred Heart Church, just several blocks from where they lived. John was involved with the Port Jervis Fire Department.

John, Jr., lived at 125 West Main Street until his death on March 9, 1916. He had retired from the Erie Railroad in 1915 "after he was taken ill with blood poisoning from which he never recovered." He committed suicide almost one year after the death of his wife and forced retirement, by hanging himself. His wife Mary had died March 18, 1915 and according to her obituary, on account of her "amiable character left behind many sincere friends." She was also active in church affairs. She left behind three sisters: Mrs. Thomas W. Lyons, Mrs. Anna J. Madigan and Mrs. Ella Dow, as well as three children.

By the marriage of
John, Jr. and Mary there were
three children: John Cannon
(1872-1880?), James Cannon
(1875-1948) and Nell Cannon
(1878-1965). For one year,
1886, John Cannon, Jr. is listed as living at 333 Main Street,
the address of Fort Decker
before Main Street was divided into East and West Main
Streets in 1888. Also living
there at the time was Martin
Quick. James lived at 125 West
Main Street from his birth
until 1901, when he moved to
the West, and died in San
Francisco.

Courtesy Minisink Valley Historical Society

James Cannon

Nell was a clerk at the First National Bank in Port Jervis,
and lived at 125 West Main Street until at least 1917. By 1922 she
was living elsewhere in the city. Nell Cannon was a lifelong resident of Port Jervis and a member of St. Mary's Church, the
Catholic Daughters of America, and the Port Jervis Democratic
Party. She lived at 15 Broome Street where she died.

As the years passed, the Cannon family rented the stone
house out to a number of families. They included C. L. Barkman
in 1887 and Patrick Noonan, a brakeman for the Erie Railroad,
who lived there for several years beginning in 1892, and left
sometime before 1897. The family most associated with the

house in modern times, and who lived in the house longer than any other family, the Campfield family, moved into the house sometime before 1900.

Beginning in 1875, John Cannon, Sr. began a process in which the "Stone House Property" he had purchased in 1865 was subdivided. The first property, present-day 133 West Main Street, was sold to his daughter Catherine (Cannon) Caufield, who in turn sold it to her brother, John, Jr. In 1890, James Eagen purchased the property and built a house on the lot in 1898. This house passed through a series of owners and was ultimately purchased by the Minisink Valley Historical Society in 1981. It was later demolished because of its derelict condition.

In 1915, John Cannon, Jr., who had obtained the title to the remaining properties from his parents, transferred his interests in them to his daughter Nell Cannon. In 1923 Nell divested herself of two of the remaining three properties. The parcel at 131 West Main Street, along with its 1892 Queen Anne-styled Victorian house constructed by John Cannon, Jr., was sold to John and Lauretta Connelly in 1923. They sold it to William and Mildred McCann in 1946, who in turn left it to Peter and Linda (McCann) Kowal in 1979. The Kowals sold the property to the Minisink Valley Historical Society in 1980. The house is now home to the offices of the Society; purchased with funds from a bequest by the late Robert Kleinstuber, an active member of the Society, the house was subsequently named the Robert Kleinstuber House in his memory.

In 1923, Nell Cannon also sold the 125 West Main property to Cinderella Bauch and Mary Cherry. The house at 125 West Main Street no longer stands but passed through a number of owners until it was purchased by Anna and George Greiner in 1945. Mr. Greiner was well known for his beautiful gardens, and after Fort Decker was taken over by the Society, he cared for its grounds until he died. He was assisted by Mr. and Mrs. William McCann, residents of 131 West Main. A World War I veteran, Greiner was always proud of the flagpole that stands to the western side of Fort Decker, and many long-time residents will remember his patriotic letters to the editor in the local newspaper.

After 1923, the only property that remained in the Cannon family's ownership was Fort Decker. Here again an additional genealogy overview is needed to explain the next series of property transactions. Mary Ryan, the wife of John Cannon, Jr. had three sisters. One of her sisters, Margaret Ryan married Thomas W. Lyons. Of their four children only Lauretta Lyons and James Francis Lyons play a role in the history of Fort Decker. Lauretta moved to New York City, where she was a teacher in the Bronx. When she died Lauretta was buried in St. Mary's Cemetery in Port Jervis. Thomas W. Lyons had a brother, James H. Lyons, who married Anna Tracy. They had four children; only Mary Gertrude Lyons Kellam was involved with the estates of both Nell Cannon and Lauretta Lyons.

In 1937 Nell Cannon created a new deed for the property that added Anna Balmos as a joint tenant.. The deed was not recorded until 1944. Nell and Anna were friends; Nell even boarded with the Balmoses. In October 1958 Anna Balmos died; in November 1958 Nell Cannon then entered into joint tenancy with Lauretta Lyons, a first cousin. Nell Cannon died on September 5, 1965 at the age of 80, and is buried in an

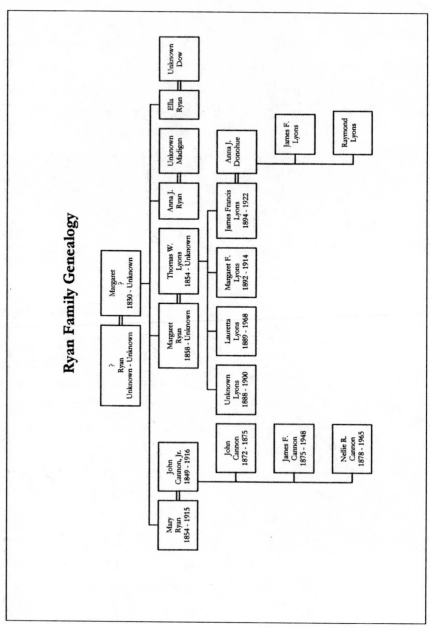

Courtesy Nancy Conod and Nancy Vocci

The Mary Ryan family genealogy

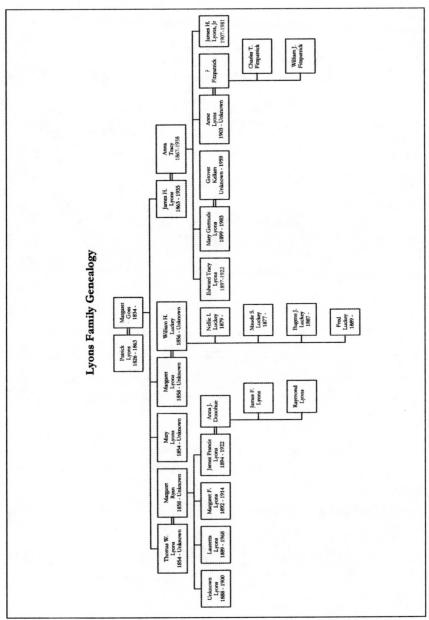

Courtesy Nancy Conod and Nancy Vocci

The Lyons and Kellam family genealogy

Courtesy Minisink Valley Historical Society

Fort Decker, c. 1900

unmarked grave at St. Mary's Cemetery in Port Jervis. She is next to her long-time friend Anna Balmos, also in an unmarked grave.

Nell left Lauretta Lyons the sole owner of the property and the administratrix of her will. In the petition for administration of her estate, the application stated that the stone house had "great historic value to the community" and was worth $3,000. Upon the death of Lauretta Lyons on March 3, 1968, the property was inherited by her nephews James and Raymond Lyons. They were the sons of her brother James Francis Lyons and his wife Anna J. Donohue Lyons. The administratrix of Lauretta Lyon's will was her first cousin Gertrude Lyons Kellam. On April 27, 1970, acting in her role as administratrix, Gertrude Kellam sold the building to the Minisink Valley Historical Society for $1,000 with the support of Lauretta Lyon's nephews.

THE DECKER STONE HOUSE
IN THE TWENTIETH CENTURY

For more than fifty years, beginning sometime after 1900, members of the Campfield family resided at Fort Decker. John Wesley Campfield (1828-1905) and his wife Sarah M. Campfield (1864-1956) lived in the old stone house with their two sons, Charles Moses Campfield (1888-1971) and H. Stanley Campfield (1894-1903). John Campfield's occupation is listed as a farmer, and he was a Civil War veteran, having served in the 101st NY Volunteer Infantry. He was a member of the local Carroll GAR Post No. 279, a veteran's organization.

Federal census records state that Sarah Campfield was born in Pennsylvania, while her obituary says that she was born in Bevans, New Jersey. She was the daughter of Aaron and Sarah Ann Hedgeland Hungerford. She lived for a few years in Scotchtown, New York, near Middletown, before moving to Port Jervis and into the stone house in 1900. Mrs. Campfield was well known in the West End neighborhood where she lived for five decades. A member of the West End Reformed Church, she was one of the oldest living members of the Ladies Aid organization of the church. Her funeral services were held at the stone

Courtesy Minisink Valley Historical Society

The family most associated with Fort Decker in modern times is the Campfields. They are pictured here in 1948 from left: Flojean Campfield (Collette), Sarah M. Campfield, Minnie Dewey Campfield and Charles Moses Campfield.

house, and many of her neighbors came to pay their respects. Her obituary said she was well-liked and respected.

    Charles, known as "Mose," married Minnie Dewey (1902-1975) in 1939, and from that marriage there was a daughter, Flojean, who lived in the stone house until her graduation from high school in 1949. Flojean was named for the well-known eatery that still operates along the Delaware River in Port Jervis. She maintains an active interest in the Society's operations, and provided important research materials for this book.

She is the last child to have
lived in the stone house.

Charles Campfield was
born in Mast Hope,
Pennsylvania and served over-
seas with the 51st Pioneer
Infantry in World War I. He
returned home to work in the
Knickerbocker Silver Plate
factory, the Brox & Ryall glass
house and then as a box pack-
er and inspector for the Erie
Railroad. He retired in 1957
after 49 years of service. He is
often remembered for the bib
overalls he wore.

Minnie Campfield was
born in Unadilla, New York,
the daughter of Lee and Alice
Dewey, and lived in a house in
Port Jervis that fronted Union

Courtesy Minisink Valley Historical Society

*Charles Campfield in his World War
I uniform.*

Street and intersected with Ferry Street. She worked at various
times as an operator for the Little Tots Dress Co., Gillinder
Glass Company, and for the well-known local photographer Gus
Krauss. From a previous marriage there were three sons:
Richard Teller, Gerald Teller and Robert Teller Bernhardt. The
three boys never lived at Fort Decker but were adopted by other
families and lived in New Jersey.

The Campfields were private people, and few of the

Courtesy Minisink Valley Historical Society

Flojean Campfield Collette in front of Fort Decker in 1942.

neighbors ever saw the inside of the house when they lived there. They moved from the house at least twice, once during Charles Campfield's military service during World War I and again in 1924. By 1926, they were back in the house that would be home to them for years to come.

Several stories have been passed down from the Campfield residency. The first concerns an alligator that was said to be kept behind Fort Decker. A visitor once said that he distinctly remembered that Mose Campfield had kept the alligator in a barrel, and when it got too big, Campfield released it into the Delaware River. The visitor showed the writer where the location was, and unknown to the visitor, it corresponded exactly to where the remains of a barrel had been discovered in the herb garden during archaeological excavations.

Another humorous story, although it involves a sad moment for the family, took place at the wake of Sarah Campfield in December 16, 1956. The wake was held in the parlor room of the structure, and the lid of the coffin was held open with a pole or stick. Attached to the lid was a floral piece. Local police officer and neighbor Bud Coslick came into the room to pay his respects. He stepped on a loose floor board and the other end popped up and jarred the floral piece from the lid. The piece then fell onto Mrs. Campfield's face, startling everyone who was in the room. Coslick went over to the coffin, reattached the floral piece and paid his respects.

In October, 1958, Charles and Minnie Campfield retired and moved to Lake Helen, Florida. Daughter Flojean married, and continues to live in the area near her family. All of the deceased family members are buried in Laurel Grove Cemetery in Port Jervis. The building was never occupied again and was listed as vacant in succeeding city directories.

During the period the Campfields lived in the stone house a bathroom, electricity and natural gas were installed. The house did not have hot water or a central heating system until after 1970. Kerosene heaters and wood stoves provided heat for the building, and a Swinton stove was used for cooking in the kitchen. The entire stone exterior of the building was repointed, and the wood trim painted black during this time.

Newspaper clippings and photographs show the yard was well kept and that large vines grew at both ends of the building. Longtime residents remember that the Campfields grew a tropical plant called a night-blooming cereus in a large tub that was kept in the hall. On the one night of the year it bloomed, the plant was brought outside and people from all over the neighborhood came to see this phenomenon.

In June, 1903, the original 1793 roof of the building was taken off by William Wilkins, a local contractor, and some of the hand-wrought nails were displayed at the offices of a local newspaper, the Port Jervis *Union*. The roof that was installed by

Wilkins may be the one under the current roof. Another article in July, 1903 stated that John Cannon was considering removing the large datestone to see if any historical material was contained within. Whether this was ever done is unknown, but it seems unlikely because of the size of the stone, and because datestones from that time period were generally made of solid blocks.

It was also in 1903 that the most dramatic and well-documented story since Brant's raid in 1779 affected a family that lived in the stone house. On August 16, 1903, the Campfield family, who had traveled with the family of George Hornbeck to their summer home at Westcolong Pond in Pike County, suffered a great tragedy. Sarah Campfield was a housekeeper for the Hornbecks, and other local families. The children of both families, including Stanley Campfield and Jacob Hornbeck, often played together at Westcolong Pond. According to family members, Stanley Campfield was sitting in a hammock on the front porch of the building and further along on the porch, leaning against the house, was a loaded Flobert rifle. It fell over, for reasons still unknown, and went off, the bullet hitting Stanley in the neck.

The first newspaper account of the accident reported the tragedy a little differently. This account states that Elmer Hornbeck, an older brother to Jacob Hornbeck, "returned from a trip on the lake and placed a Flobert rifle on the front porch of the house where the campers were staying. During his absence Jacob Hornbeck took the gun and loaded it with a cartridge he found somewhere and was shooting it for fun. As the weapon was discharged, Canfield (sic) went around the corner of the house and caught the bullet in the back of his neck."

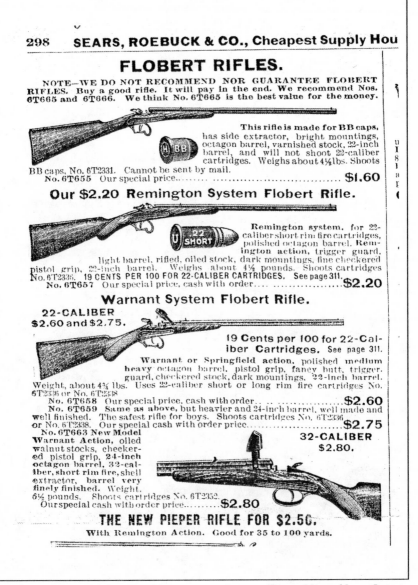

Courtesy Mim and James Carpenter

*An ad from the Sears Roebuck catalog illustrates how common and cheap
a Flobert rifle was at the time of the shooting of Stanley Campfield.*

A second story appeared on September 29, 1903, and states that while sitting in the hammock eating a piece of cake, Stanley was struck in the back of his head by a rifle ball that was "accidentally discharged by his companion who had taken the gun." There are other versions of how the incident occurred that differ greatly from the family's and the reporter's recollections. Jacob Hornbeck remembered both may have been playing with the rifle. He thought that he and Stanley did not know it was loaded. Another story passed down is that they were shooting rattlesnakes. Finally, it has been suggested that Hornbeck tripped with the gun in his hand and it went off.

Whatever happened, the gun discharged and Stanley Campfield was shot in the neck. At the time it was considered only a flesh wound, in fact the newspaper reported that the boy

Courtesy Peter Osborne

The note on the right side of this post card of Fort Decker describes the tragedy of the Campfield shooting. The name is misspelled on the card.

would improve and recover quickly. The boy was taken inside the house and a doctor called. At some point he began to lose feeling in his legs and body, his vision was impaired and, according to Jacob Hornbeck, he was in great pain. He was brought to the Port Jervis Hospital and the bullet was removed. But, because the bullet had been in his neck too long, recovery was impossible. He lingered for about six weeks until he died on September 28, 1903 at

Courtesy Minisink Valley Historical Society

Stanley Campfield

the age of eight. His obituary is sad to read; it says "he was a bright, lovable little fellow."

The tragedy was an enormous one for both families. The Hornbecks offered to pay the medical costs and funeral expenses, and the Campfields agreed. A plot was purchased at Laurel Grove Cemetery in Port Jervis, a service was held at Fort Decker, and a headstone erected. With that, everyone thought it was the end of the story - that is, until the early 1970s, when the Society purchased the building. In the process of cleaning it out, a volunteer found a fragment of bone, perhaps from Stanley's skull, wrapped in a piece of cheesecloth.

At the time, no one knew the significance of that discovery. When the author began to research the tragedy, it was discovered that Sarah Campfield had kept a small fragment of bone from Stanley. In the years following that sad event she regularly held seances in the kitchen room of the Fort, and tried to contact her dead son. This piece of evidence only makes the whole story more mysterious because one has to wonder where that piece of bone came from, and how it was acquired. Family members believe that the bullet that hit Stanley shattered his skull, and that this fragment was a piece that fell out. A portion of the skull may have also been removed to relieve pressure on the brain, a medical practice for more than one hundred years.

To add even more to the mystery, when a family member was buried next to Stanley Campfield in the 1950s, the grave digger mistakenly dug into Stanley's grave. He was not able to find any remains of Stanley -- no coffin, no metal hinges, or even human remains. So, if Stanley Campfield was not buried at Laurel Grove Cemetery, where was he buried?

The author interviewed Jacob Hornbeck in the 1980s and even though he was in his nineties, he could still recall the event. He was puzzled by the idea of an empty grave because he remembered his father having paid for the funeral and medical costs. Hornbeck thought the Campfields were a little strange, and said that Mrs. Campfield, who had always been fond of him, never treated him the same after that tragic day. He did not think it impossible that Stanley may have been buried in the basement of Fort Decker.

When archaeologists were conducting test pits in the basement of the building in 1998 and 1999 they were specifically directed to dig in a place where the floor seemed to have a hollow sound when struck. Nothing was found at that location, and so the mystery remains. Perhaps Stanley Campfield's remains were decomposed, and nothing remained of him. After all, it had been more than ninety years since he died. Flojean Campfield Collette did confirm that Sarah Campfield held seances in the building, and had once found an object wrapped in cloth in her mother's jewelry box. Her mother told her to never touch it again because it was a bone fragment from Stanley Campfield.

Another memorable event during the early twentieth century was a fire in the kitchen that could have destroyed the structure. On January 22, 1924, a spark ignited in the chimney from a kitchen range and landed on the wooden lintel of the old fire-

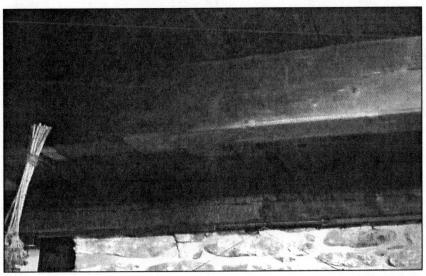

Courtesy Peter Osborne

The fire of 1924 quickly burned through the plaster ceiling and seared the beams and second story floorboards. If the fire had not been discovered when it was, the whole building might have been destroyed.

place. The fire spread slowly and crept through the space between the plaster ceiling and floorboards of the second floor.

Neighbors saw great quantities of smoke coming out of the main (north) chimney, and a policeman investigating the scene found the house filled with smoke. After firemen arrived, the fire was quickly extinguished. In the process, the front of the fireplace, mantelpiece, floor boards and second floor joists were destroyed. At the time, the house was occupied by Mr. and Mrs. Jerry Winters, who were getting ready to move to a new house they were constructing in the Brooklyn section of Port Jervis near the route of the D and H Canal. The reporter also noted the Winters family did not have any insurance to cover the damage.

FORT DECKER AS A MUSEUM

There was interest in the local community to preserve Fort Decker as a historic site beginning in the late 1880s. In 1893, the centennial of the reconstruction of the building, a newspaper article recounted the history of the building. During this time there was discussion proposing the building be given or sold to the newly-formed Minisink Valley Historical Society. The article challenged the Society to purchase the historic structure so its growing collection of artifacts, documents and books could be properly stored. Material for the article was provided by Rev. Samuel W. Mills, who had been the pastor of the Dutch Reformed Church of Deerpark (1857-1871). He was also the President of the Minisink Valley Historical Society (1889-1902) and the son-in-law of Stephen St. John.

The Machackemech Chapter of the Daughters of the Revolution (*not to be confused with a similar organization, the Daughters of the American Revolution*) placed a tablet commemorating the history of the Fort on the front of the building on May 16, 1908. The plaque was unveiled by Miss Agnes Van Noy in a special ceremony conducted by members of the organization after per-

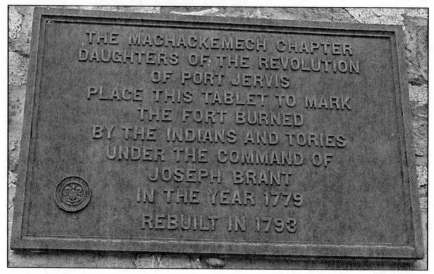

This plaque was placed on the southeastern corner of Fort Decker by the local chapter of the Daughters of the Revolution in 1908.

mission was granted by the Cannon family. Also in attendance were city and school officials, students, members of the Minisink Valley Historical Society and the general public. Two of the more interesting attendees were members of the Daughters of the Revolution who had long associations with the building: Mrs. Samuel W. Mills, who was born there, and Mrs. Frederick W. Best, whose grandmother, Mrs. John Decker, had been born there.

The organization had previously assisted in the general cleanup of the historic Machackemeck churchyard on East Main Street in 1907. Part of that project included marking the known Revolutionary War soldier's graves with new monuments, including that of Martinus Decker. They also erected a new memorial commemorating Cole's Fort and the church at the edge of the churchyard.

The organization also made an effort in the early 1920s to purchase Fort Decker from Nell Cannon, proposing to preserve it as a museum. Cannon was not willing to sell the home of her father and grandfather but she did think she might make it available to the group in years to come. Another tradition has it that she wanted to keep the property in her family for one hundred years, something she ultimately accomplished.

On October 2, 1937, Mrs. Frederick W. Best, a Decker descendant, and participant in the unveiling of the Daughters of the Revolution plaque almost thirty years before, unveiled the new state education historic marker that currently stands on the

Courtesy Peter Osborne

The New York State historic marker was placed in 1936 and is incorrect in one fact: John Jervis, while staying at the St. John Hotel on occasion, did not use the building as his headquarters during the construction of the canal. Rather, his office was in Mamakating, New York.

property. It was placed in front of the building, but it is said that Moses Campfield was so upset about the marker being placed in his front yard that he moved it across the street to the present-day Rose Garden. It was not until after 1960 that it was placed in its current location, on the western side yard of the building.

In 1966, discussion about purchasing the Fort for a museum was again raised by the Port Jervis Garden Club in a local newspaper article, along with the idea of creating a city memorial to John B. Jervis at the site. Among the people at the meeting where this was discussed were future MVHS board member Edwin Dietz and D. Nelson Raynor, the editor of the *Union Gazette*, the city historian, and MVHS member.

In the summer of 1969 a series of conversations led to the purchase of the building by the Society. It is through the friendship of Society President Cornelius Cuddeback with Gertrude Kellam that the possibility was first discussed and ultimately came to pass. In addition, William Gregg, a local attorney, who had been involved with the Society and administering both the Cannon and Lyons estates, assisted in the negotiations.

At a special meeting of the directors of the Society on July 16, 1969, a proposal to purchase Fort Decker was discussed. There was considerable and heated debate as to whether to keep the building or deed it over to the city of Port Jervis. In the end it was resolved by the members that the Society should purchase the structure and retain it.

Within a week an offer was made to Gertude Kellam to purchase the stone house. The Society finally acquired the old stone house on April 27, 1970, for $1,000 after decades of discussions. The acquisition was made with the proceeds of the

sale of property that had been
previously bequeathed to the
Society in 1961 by member
Mary Cole Hetzel Miller. It
was all the money the Society
had. The transaction was handled pro bono on behalf of
the Society by Richard Walker,
Esq., a member and local
attorney.

A ceremony was held
to commemorate the turning
over of the keys from
Gertrude Kellam to Calvin
Crane, then President of the
Minisink Valley Historical
Society. There was much
interest in the larger Orange

Courtesy Minisink Valley Historical Society

Society President Calvin Van Etten Crane taking the keys for Fort Decker from Gertrude Kellam.

County history community, as the purchase of the building was
featured in the Orange County Community of Museums and
Galleries quarterly magazine, *Museum Matters,* in the summer
issue of 1970. The building was nominated for, and subsequently listed on, the United States Department of the Interior's
National Register of Historic Places on June 13, 1974. A formal
dedication took place on July 22, 1974.

It was suggested by the Orange County Community of
Museums and Galleries that the Society undertake a complete
study of the building that included investigating the history of
the structure, and then consider possible uses. Restoration sce-

narios included the restoration of the building to its 1793 condition, or restoring the exterior, but renovating the interior for
contemporary purposes. It is not known if the comprehensive
study was ever done. The author has concluded that it was not
completed. However the Society, on three different occasions,
did have experts come to Fort Decker and evaluate the building.

The first expert to visit was Roy Vail, a well-known figure
in Orange County historical circles who came to Fort Decker
sometime in 1971 and provided the Society with an analysis of
the various periods that were represented architecturally. Vail
presented his findings to the Society in a letter and later, in 1972,
donated a Dutch door that he hoped would be used to replace
the front door of the building. The door was not used for that
purpose but the Society still retains it.

One of his recommendations was that the partitions on

Courtesy Minisink Valley Historical Society

Fort Decker, c. 1970

the first floor be retained and that the shed on the back of the building, now the bathroom, be removed. Another expert, Kenneth Hasbrouck, a member of the Society, and President of the Huguenot Historical Society, also provided expertise to the Society, although no written copy of his recommendations survives.

Board member Robert Kleinstuber, along with other members of the Society and the community, provided funds that allowed cleanup work to be done in the fall of 1971. This included closing the northern cellar entrance, repair work to the chimneys, and the installation of the two bluestone caps.

In the next few years, work on the first floor of the building continued, including the removal of wall partitions on the first floor, installation of a new electric service and burglar alarm system. A new window was installed in the parlor room on the back side as well as a new bathroom, sink, and roof. Much of the work was undertaken by local contractors George Wilson and Peter McCoy.

During these efforts a controversy ensued when member Mrs. Charles Prussia demanded that she be placed in charge of the restoration of the building. While it is not known what the outcome was, she was probably unhappy with the progress, or the kinds of projects that were being undertaken. She had the support of Robert Kleinstuber, and she was said to be very knowledgeable about old buildings. The details of a series of letters and phone calls between her and the Society board members between the fall of 1971 and spring of 1972 are not known. Ultimately, the Society's board did not allow her to take over the project, and continued on its course.

Unfortunately there are few photographs that exist to document what the interior of the building looked like before the work was started. Because there are no records existing of the pre-existing conditions, one can only make assumptions, based on paint shadows, trim marks, and the few recollections that have been passed down.

The interior walls of both the parlor and kitchen, with early twentieth century wallpaper still on them, were simply plastered over. The parlor room, which was actually divided into two rooms, perhaps during the 1820s, was returned to its original 1793 configuration. The wall that had previously divided the western third of the room from the main room was removed. The shadow of the divider can still be seen on the floor.

A plaster ceiling, along with the lath which had been installed on the second floor beams, also in the 1820s, was presumably removed at this time as well. The exposed surface of the second floor beams in the parlor room, which apparently had been damaged or changed, were covered over with a veneer that attempted to recreate the original beading. A floor covering, perhaps green linoleum, was removed, because small fragments of it can still be seen.

The rear window in the parlor room must have served as a storage area at one point, perhaps when the wooden frame addition was still attached to the main building, because paint shadows can still be seen in the casing. While the casings for both windows in each room are believed to be original, the sashes are not. The oldest remaining sash in the building is in the rear window of the kitchen.

The mantle in the parlor, which was broken into many

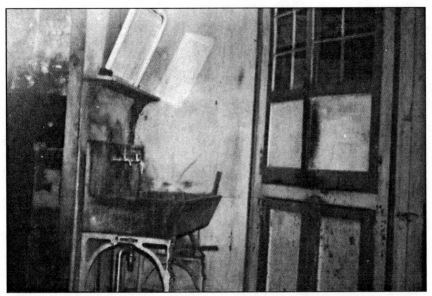

Courtesy Minisink Valley Historical Society

One of the few known views of the interior of Fort Decker prior to its purchase by the Society in 1970. This view is looking toward the northeastern corner of the building. The original Decker cupboard is to the right.

pieces, was removed in 1972 and placed in the basement. It was restored and painted by the author in the early 1980s. The fireplace's interior stone walls were repointed during the 1970s, although the shadows from the original wood paneling can still be seen on the ceiling-side second floor beams. Stovepipe holes were all closed up. Wallboard was removed from the hallway on the south side and plastered over.

The kitchen area had been altered substantially over the years. In 1793, the room was originally configured as it is now. The fireplace was plastered on three sides with a simple wooden mantle. A small sample of the plaster still remains near the joining of the second floor and fireplace on the south side. Inside the fireplace was a bake oven that was subsequently removed. Pieces of the exterior section of the oven occasionally turn up when frost heaves the soil. It is believed that the fireplace may have been closed off when cast-iron stoves became popular. Coal became readily available with the construction of the D and H canal in the 1820s. The stove was then probably placed directly in front of the closed fireplace.

Flojean Campfield Collette remembers that the kitchen was actually three rooms. A bathroom was located near the side window; the kitchen area included the fireplace, a small pantry and sink, where the corner cupboard is currently. The third room, a bedroom, was to the left of the entrance as you come into the room.

Some time between 1970 and 1980, the Society installed a sink on the western wall which has subsequently been covered over and used as exhibit space. Behind the sink is the only surviving section of the exterior wall, with the original plastering and wallpaper intact exactly as it was. Two openings were cut into the dividing walls in the kitchen at that time to allow visitors to see the construction techniques of the eighteenth century. The main stone fireplace was repointed, but left unplastered and without a lintel.

New electricity was installed throughout the building and plain light fixtures were installed in critical locations. All of the first-floor rooms have been painted several times since 1980.

The second floor was essentially left intact, perhaps because the Society did not have adequate funding to press on with additional projects. The mantle that enhances the second-floor fireplace was also found in the basement, restored and

THIS HOUSE WAS OCCUPIED FOR ONE HUNDRED YEARS (1865-1965) BY THE FAMILY OF NELLIE R. CANNON. THROUGH THE EFFORTS OF GERTRUDE LYONS KELLAM, THIS SITE WAS MADE AVAILABLE TO THE MINISINK VALLEY HISTORICAL SOCIETY IN 1970.

Courtesy Peter Osborne

This plaque was installed and dedicated on July 19, 1981 to honor the owners and the people who made the sale of Fort Decker to the Society possible. Unfortunately the plaque contains several inaccuracies.

reinstalled. The chimney was re-plastered and painted. The hall and two southern rooms on the second floor have also been painted.

Exterior projects have included the removal of two large trees, one a large maple that was located near the current historic marker. It had grown so large that it covered a portion of the southern side of the roof. The maple was removed sometime between 1966 and 1970. A hemlock tree growing at the southwestern corner of the building was also removed sometime after 1980.

After the work of the 1970s was completed, the building was opened to the public by Society members, and members of the Old Mine Road Chapter of the Daughters of the American

Revolution, for special occasions, particularly the annual com-
memoration of the Battle at Minisink. Items were brought from
the Society's library archives to be displayed at the Fort, and
members of the Old Mine Road Chapter cleaned the building
annually, opened it to the public on occasion, and held meetings
there.

With the hiring of the Society's first full-time executive
director in 1980, the Board, under the leadership of Charles H.
Swartwout, Jr. began developing long-range goals for Fort
Decker and the surrounding properties. In late 1980, the Society
began a series of property acquisitions to enhance Fort Decker
and to provide additional resources for the Society. The first
property was located at 131 West Main Street, and was purchased on October 6, 1980. It was determined that it would be
used as a preservation center, a storage area and as the executive

Courtesy Peter Osborne

Fort Decker Compound, 1982

Courtesy Peter Osborne

The Robert Kleinstuber House, c. 1984

director's residence.

This building, an 1892 Queen Anne Victorian-style residence, was dedicated to the memory of Robert Kleinstuber, a former board member, who left the Society a substantial financial contribution in 1977. The Robert Kleinstuber House has been the focus of much effort since its purchase. The exterior of the Kleinstuber House was initially restored in 1983, and subsequently renovated again in 1996. Throughout the 1990s the interior of the building was renovated, with the remaining historic features of the building being preserved. In the fall of 1999 the entire second floor was renovated to serve as the Director's residence.

On December 7, 1981, the society purchased 133 West

Courtesy Peter Osborne

Educational programs have been conducted regularly at Fort Decker since its purchase in 1970.

Main Street, adjacent to the Kleinstuber House, and in 1987 purchased the 125 West Main Street property on the north side of Fort Decker. Both properties had derelict buildings on them. Because they were badly deteriorated, they were demolished in an effort to create additional protective buffer space around the Fort and to allow more on-site programs. William Bavoso, Esq., a local attorney and member of the Board of Directors handled all of the property transactions pro bono for the Society. The Fort Decker Compound, as it is now known, has become the center for many of the Society's programs.

The next step in the long-range plan was to develop the property as an historic site and base for its educational programs; since then a number of projects have been undertaken. First, the building was opened to the public on a regular basis in

1981 for the summer months and Christmas season. This practice has continued to the present time.

Second, during the 1980s, work began to implement the
plan. Fort Decker's interior and exterior, which had not been
painted in decades, was painted, and the building's interior was
repaired. A new aluminum flagpole was donated and installed by
the members of the Tri-State Naval Ship Post #7241, and dedicated on July 18, 1982. In the last few years a new electric service, heating, ventilation and air conditioning systems, smoke and
burglar alarms and new track lighting were installed along with a
new parking area and a boundary fence. Most recently, a site
evaluation was completed to be sure the programs offered met
the standards as defined by the Americans With Disabilities Act.

A third goal was to undertake new research on the history of the building and its inhabitants. For the third time an architectural expert was brought to the site. In 1980, Donald
Carpentier, owner of Eastfield Village, a recreated late eighteenth century community, met with Society officials. He was
critical of the work done in the previous decade, saying that the
"building was left in a state in which it never existed prior to the
'restoration effort.'" One of his most important recommendations was that "The house should be interpreted as an architectural artifact and used as an exhibit space and not a Doll House!"
He provided the Society with a list of projects, some of which
were completed. He also provided the Society with a proposal to
undertake some restoration work.

Results of this considerable research are a 1993 Heritage
Days booklet entitled **The Port Jervis Area Heritage
Commission Salutes The Decker Stone House 1793-1993**,

Courtesy Minisink Valley Historical Society

Over the last three decades hundreds of school children and thousands of visitors have visited Fort Decker to see what life was like in an earlier time.

and this manuscript. A series of exhibits on the building have been upgraded regularly since they were first unveiled in 1982. Exhibits have focused on the building's history during the Revolutionary War era, and the Delaware and Hudson Canal period. Other temporary exhibits have also been undertaken including shows on quilts, summer activities in the 1800s, the restoration of the Statue of Liberty, and lifestyles of the eighteenth century. One of the more interesting displays is the cutaway of the wall in the kitchen where the original lath and plaster construction using hay and Delaware River mud can be seen.

In 1982, archaeological testing was conducted by the Orange County Chapter of the New York Archaeological Association in the area now occupied by the herb garden. This excavation provided evidence of lifestyles from the late nineteenth century. In 2000, the organization returned to do additional testing in the basement of the building, as well as several locations on the exterior of the building.

Around the grounds, an herb garden was planted behind the Fort. In the summer of 1989, tree seedlings from historic sites around the country were planted on the two open lots, creating an historic tree grove. In 2002 the Society's volunteers and director began to undertake eighteenth-century cooking demonstrations in a fire pit constructed on the grounds. In 2004 an heirloom garden was created using seeds obtained from historic sites with historically correct gardens.

A number of historic artifacts have been installed on the grounds as well. Four millstones that were going to be discarded by their owners have been given to the Society and placed on

Courtesy Peter Osborne

The Society's heirloom garden surrounded by a rabbit fencing that was commonly used to keep pests from the garden.

our property. The two millstones on the outer corners of the property were discovered in a bank of old fill on Barcelow Street in Port Jervis. The millstone in the center of the property was from the old Space mill in Huguenot. The fourth millstone, now located by the herb garden, was found at the Terbell mill site, located behind the Port Jervis Free Library, during excavations creating the parking lot. This stone is interesting because of its color, indicating that it may have originally been quarried near Riverdale, *(Passaic County)* New Jersey. The snubbing post and stepping stone in front of the Kleinstuber House were taken from a historic house that was demolished where the horse farm is located in Huguenot at the junction of Horn Road and Route 209.

A D and H canal snubbing post that was moved from a private residence in Huguenot, New York, is now located in the back corner of the property. It is not known where it was originally sited on the canal, but it is numbered "115," designating that it was sited along the main line of the Erie Railroad near Shohola, Pennsylvania. There is speculation that the snubbing post probably came from the canal somewhere between Lackawaxen and Honesdale, Pennsylvania.

In the years since the purchase of the building, thousands of visitors have come to Fort Decker to participate in programs, view exhibits and watch demonstrations. Visitors have included school children, tourists, civic organizations, Society members, and area residents. The Society's founders would be proud that their vision of 1889, the year it was created, has largely been accomplished, and strongly continues.

Who Turns On The Lights at 9:15?

One of the most frequently asked questions visitors have is: Is the Decker stone house haunted, and if so by whom? About fifteen years ago the Director, and subsequently, a Society volunteer, revealed they felt rushes of cold air going up the staircase when they were turning off the lights on the second floor. Neither told the other about what they had experienced. This phenomenon only happened at night, and because the building is very drafty, particularly during the winter, both thought there might be a simple explanation - a door or window that was slightly ajar, or perhaps a gusty wind. Those items were checked and did not seem to be the source of the drafts.

When a new motion-sensing light system was installed on the first floor of the building in 1993, a different phenomenon began. Very soon after the installation was complete, the lights in both the parlor room and kitchen would go on automatically without anyone being in the building. It was noted that the lights were going on regularly, between 9:00 and 10:00 p.m. each evening. First the track lighting in the parlor room would go on, then about fifteen seconds later the kitchen lights would go on.

The contractor who installed the system tested it, and found no problems. He explained that the system's method of operation is based on heat and motion, and it would take an object the size of a small child or dog to set the system off.

The Director looked for other plausible explanations, including the possibility that it might be the headlights of automobiles turning down Old West Main Street setting off the system. However, the lights continued to go on, even when there were no cars going down the street. The lights went on occasionally during the daytime. All of this occurs while a security alarm system, equally sensitive to noise and motion, does not register any alarms. There are no plausible reasons why this should happen. At least one psychic has visited the building, and reported that terrible things happened there.

In October, 2001, Linda Zimmerman, an active researcher of the spiritual world, visited Fort Decker to undertake a study. Her belief is that there is more to a person than a physical body, and that the spirit contained within all people is released when a person dies. She argues that sometimes spirits find themselves caught between worlds, because a common thread that runs through hauntings are suicides, anger, hatred, grief, regret and guilt. Finally, she believes that there is no such thing as a happy ghost; rather, it is a spirit confused by something that happened in its previous life.

Zimmerman's visit brought a serious interest in spiritual matters that had never been undertaken at the Fort. She used a Sony camcorder with a Nightshot feature that allows one to record in infrared in complete darkness. On the day Zimmerman visited only one piece of "proof" was captured on film: an orb appears in one of the photographs taken. Zimmerman was sitting in the parlor room, and an orb appears floating in the room. It is believed that "orbs," or the circular shapes that are occasionally seen in photographs, represent a "spirit" from times past. At the moment the photographer took the picture he felt there was a presence in the room.

Other interesting readings occurred on that evening with an EMF meter and a non-contact thermometer. High readings that came and went were noted near the fireplace and the corner cupboard. It should be noted that the main electric service comes into the building near this corner of the building. Infrared footage was later analyzed, and showed that a white light darted in front of the camera and was gone.

Speculation has centered on Sarah Campfield as being

Courtesy Linda Zimmerman

Linda Zimmerman and Michael Worden creating a video of their research findings at Fort Decker. An orb can be seen at the center of the photograph.

the possible spirit roaming the building. She went to bed about 9:30 p.m. every evening, going from room to room before retiring to her bedroom. There were of course the tragic events that had happened while the family was living there, including the death of her son Stanley. Mrs. Campfield died in the building,

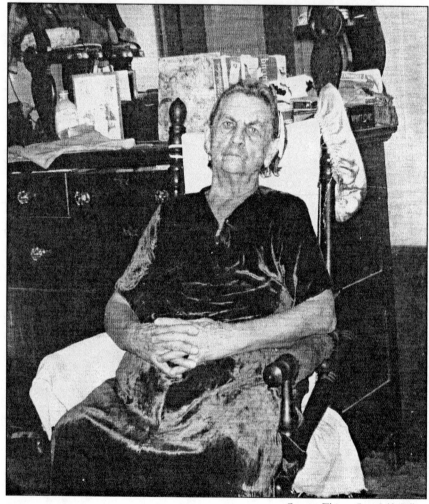

Courtesy Flojean Campfield Collette

Sarah Campfield

and her wake was conducted in the parlor room. She was then interred at Laurel Grove Cemetery, along with other family members.

Another possibility is that this spirit may be Stanley Campfield, the young boy killed in 1903. Or it could be the spirit of Elizabeth Brink Drake (1723-1798), whose childhood was a traumatic one. Her mother died when she was very young, and she was sent to Fort Decker to live with her aunt and uncle, Katherine Brink Decker and Richard Decker. Her father was killed by the bursting of a cannon that was fired at the Brick House in Montague, New Jersey. Upon moving to the stone house she took up spinning and weaving as a livelihood. At some undetermined time she moved from Fort Decker to live at a Judge Brink's home in Milford.

Another person who may still be on the grounds is George Griener, a World War I veteran who lived next to the Fort at 125 West Main Street. After he passed away, the new owners of that house said they saw a spectre roaming around wearing a plaid shirt, just like the ones Mr. Griener wore when he was alive. The new owners also found that the lights in their home were being switched on without their knowledge. At one point the owner, Betty Kranz, told George to stop turning on the lights because it was too expensive, and the lights stopped going on.

A final possibility is John Cannon, Jr. (1848-1916), who committed suicide in his house at 125 West Main Street in 1916, one year after his retirement. He hung himself after having contracted blood poisoning. He had lived in Fort Decker for several years.

With the building having witnessed more than two hundred and forty years of human drama, there have been many people who have passed through it having their share of joy, sadness, tragedy and happiness. No matter what one thinks of the spiritual world, evidence exists that seems to confirm these strange occurrences. To be sure, there are no answers, but one must wonder about the regularity of the lights being turned on and off.

Several years ago the Port Jervis Police regularly posted an officer across the street from the Fort in a patrol car to prevent people from going up to the closed West End bridge that was in the process of being repaired. They watched with amazement as the lights went on and off with no one entering or leaving the building. The author has since concluded that there is a presence, ghost or spirit if you will, at Fort Decker, and that it regularly turns on our lighting system but does not set off the security system. For that the author is grateful, and so are the police.

VIGILANCE AND PERSEVERANCE

Today, educational programs are regularly held at the stone house including eighteenth-century cooking demonstrations, lectures and tours. The Society continues to construct and update interpretive exhibits in and around the stone house; it also conducts special education programs that interpret the lifestyles of the past three centuries and the region's history. It is officially listed on New York State's Revolutionary War Heritage Trail.

There is, as there always is with old houses, some project to do, some maintenance that is needed, gardens to be tended or grass to be cut. However, the Society can be proud of its stewardship of the property that has witnessed so much of our region's history, and played such a significant role in the American Revolution and the construction of the Delaware and Hudson Canal.

In 1887 a newspaper reporter wrote "Looking at the venerable structure, one may safely predict its ability to withstand a siege of the elements for a hundred years to come." As the Society celebrates the 210th anniversary of the rebuilding of

Courtesy Brian Lewis

Fort Decker, 2004

Fort Decker, and undertakes its second century of service to the community, it might do well to remember Martinus Decker's personal motto, which was "Vigilance and Perseverance," two qualities that will be required to preserve and commemorate the building's history into the next century.

NOTES

ABBREVIATIONS

A Bit Of Local History - "*A Bit Of Local History:Brief Sketch of the Old Stone House in Germantown*", Port Jervis Evening Gazette, Port Jervis, NY, August 13, 1887.

FDMOHC - Fort Decker Museum of History Collection

Decker Fort Edition -"*Decker Fort Edition,*" MVHS, The Mennisienk, September 1969, (Port Jervis, NY: 1969)

History of Deerpark - **History of Deerpark in Orange County,** (Port Jervis, NY, Port Jervis Union Print and Minisink Valley Historical Society, 1890)

Museum Matters - "*Port Jervis Historians Acquire Fort Decker,*" Orange County Community of Museums and Galleries, Museum Matters, Vol. IV, No. 3, July-September 1970, (Goshen, NY: 1970).

MVHS - Minisink Valley Historical Society Collection, 138 Pike Street and 127 West Main Street, Port Jervis, New York

NARA - National Archives and Records Administration, College Park, Maryland and Washington, D.C.

Peter Decker - Theresa Coyne Strasser, *Peter Decker (ca. 1711-1773) of Sussex County, New Jersey, and Some of His Descendants,* National Genealogical Quarterly, Vol. 72, No. 4, December 1984, 244.

THE ORIGINAL PEOPLE

Native Americans had been living: Philip Lord, **Documenting Prehistoric Habitation in Your Community: A Guide For Local Historians**, New York State Museum, Circular No. 55 (Albany, NY: The University of the State of New York., 1980) 3-6.

The next group of people: Ibid., 3-6.

There is at least: Peter E. Gumaer, **A History of Deerpark in Orange County,** (Port Jervis, NY: Port Jervis Union Print and Minisink Valley Historical Society, 1890), 22-23.

THE OLD MINE ROAD: EARLY SETTLEMENT

The road allowed the creation: James P. Snell, **History of Sussex and Warren Counties, New Jersey**, (Philadelphia: Everts and Peck, 1881), 25.

THE HAYNE FAMILY

Frederick Hayne (1730?-1807), builder: "*Port Jervis Historians Acquire Fort Decker,*" Orange County Community of Museums and Galleries, Museum Matters, Vol. IV, No. 3, July-September 1970, (Goshen, NY, 1970), 1, **Hardyston Memorial, A History of the Township and The North Presbyterian Church, Hardyston, Sussex County, New Jersey,** (Newton, NJ, New Jersey *Herald Print*, 1888), 130, Haynes Archives, compiled by Kenneth Bigolin, RootsWeb.com, (April 29, 2005), Passenger and Immigration Lists Index, 1500-1900s, Ancestry.com,

(February 14, 2005).
*The couple had nine children: "Decker Fort Edition,"*MVHS, The Mennisienk, September 1969, (Port Jervis, NY, 1969), 2. In this newsletter the author states that there were only three children. In Charles Stickney's history of the Hayne family genealogy, the regional historian describes it very differently, and does not agree with the preceding genealogy. He offers an entirely different version. However, further along in his book he confirms the data presented here and adds one final child, Richard. Charles Stickney, **Squire Stickney's 1895 History of Sussex, New Jersey,** (Baltimore: Gateway Press, 1977), 28 and 30.
His will, dated January 27, 1807: Hayne Family History, Wm. J. Coulter's Wantage Recorder Collection, MVHS, p. 72, **Documents Relating To The Colonial, Revolutionary and Post-Revolutionary History of the State of New Jersey, 1st Series, Vol. XL, 1806-1809,** ed. Elmer Hutchinson, (Trenton, NJ: MacCrellish and Quigley, 1947), 164.

THE HAYNE TRADING POST

Frederick Hayne arrived: "Decker Fort, or Stone House, Built in 1793, Saved by Firemen," Port Jervis Gazette, Port Jervis, NY, January 22, 1924, 3., *Museum Matters,* 1. As in so much of what has been previously written about Fort Decker and included in this book, very little is sourced and annotated, such is the case with this citation.
A 1902 newspaper article on: Old Deerpark Days, Reformed Dutch Church of Deerpark, Church Life, Vol XV, No. 8, November 1902, (Port Jervis, NY: 1902), 3.
The Hayne trading post: "A Bit Of Local History: Brief Sketch of the

Old Stone House in Germantown", *Port Jervis Evening Gazette*, Port Jervis, NY, August 13, 1887, 1. The author of the article, the oldest known history of Fort Decker, says that his information came from a relative of one of the families and an eyewitness.
Loopholes were located throughout the building: A Bit Of Local History" 1., *Museum Matters*, 1.
The building served as a tavern: A Bit Of Local History: 1.
It was only when they were supported: Alan and Barbara Aimone, *Pre-Revolution Fortified Places of New York*, Journal of the Council of Abandoned Military Posts, Vol IX, No. 3, No. 33, Fall, 1977, Periodical, 4.

THE WESTFALL AND DECKER FAMILIES

It is now known by an incorrect name: Matamoras was not given its name until the 1840s during the Mexican War, and so the name of the Fort is incorrect.
Wilhelmus Westfall married Margaret Hayne: Decker Fort Edition, 2. In this newsletter the author states that there were only five children. The genealogy as outlined here comes from the work of William Coulter, a copy of which is in the Westfall family file in FDMOHC and Dudley Ham who prepared his family's genealogy entitled *Captain Wilhelmus Westfall 1753-1796: His Genealogical History* in 1995 and deposited at MVHS and FDMOHC. The baptismal dates of the ten children were: Cathrina (baptized September 6,1780 or October 29, 1780 - ?), Alice (or Althe) (baptized September 6, 1781 or September 6, 1782 - ?), Lydia (baptized April 20, 1784 - ?), David (1789?-?), Elizabeth (1791? -?), Apollonia (1792? - ?), Benjamin (1794? - ?), Nancy (baptized August 30, 1795 - ?), John (baptized August 30, 1795 - ?), and

James (1795? - ?).

Sometime after 1783 or 1784: The couple's children were baptized in two groupings, the first, prior to 1784 in the Mahakamack Church, and the second group, after 1795, were baptized in the Clove Church.

As part of the deposition process: A Bit Of Local History, 5.

A Dutch-English dictionary: **Dutch-English and English-Dutch Dictionary,** (New York:Van Riemsdyck Book Service, 1945), 27.

Researchers suggest that: Amelia Stickney, **That Ancient Trail: The Old Mine Road,** (Trenton, NJ, Petty Printing Company, 1942), 27, Stickney, **Squire Stickney's 1895 History of Sussex, New Jersey,** 3, Benton Weaver Decker, **The Decker Genealogy: Some Descendants of the Dutch Immigrants, Johannes Gerretsen (Decker) and Jan Broersen (Decker),** (San Diego, California: Budget Book Manufacturing Co., 1980), James Cole Decker to Charles Stickney, October 8, 1915, photocopy in FDMOHC.

Jan Decker traveled back and forth: Here again the record is complete with inconsistencies and genealogies that do not match. Stickney, **Squire Stickney's 1895 History of Sussex, New Jersey,** 6, Decker, **The Decker Genealogy: Some Descendants of the Dutch Immigrants, Johannes Gerretsen (Decker) and Jan Broersen (Decker),** 1, **Ulster County, NY, Probate Records, Vol. 1,** ed. Anjou, Gustave, (New York: Privately published, 1906), 129.

Given the accepted birth date: Decker, **The Decker Genealogy: Some Descendants of the Dutch Immigrants, Johannes Gerretsen (Decker) and Jan Broersen (Decker),** 121-122,

Theresa Coyne Strasser, *Peter Decker (ca. 1711-1773) of Sussex County, New Jersey, and Some of His Descendants,* National Genealogical Quarterly, Vol. 72, No. 4, December 1984, 244.

William J. Coulter, **Minisink and Wallkill Precinct Historical Chronicles, 1940-1962,** No. 147, 576. MVHS and FDMOHC.

Peter married Magdalena Oosterhout: Peter Decker, 244.

By Peter Decker's marriage: Decker Fort Edition, 2. In this newsletter the author states that there were twelve children, although they are not listed. *Peter Decker,* 244. Sussex Borough Tercentenary Committee, **Deckertown-Sussex Tercentenary Record: A History of Borough of Sussex, NJ,** (Newton, NJ: New Jersey Herald, 1964), 6.

The listing shows a Petris Decker: Snell, **History of Sussex and Warren Counties, New Jersey,** 30.

He was the founder: Stickney, **Squire Stickney's 1895 History of Sussex, New Jersey** 23., Snell, **History of Sussex and Warren Counties, New Jersey,** 289.

Here he built a log cabin: Snell, **History of Sussex and Warren Counties, New Jersey,** p. 289.

One puts his home at: Sussex Borough Tercentenary Committee, **Deckertown-Sussex Tercentenary Record: A History of Borough of Sussex, NJ,** 5.

A businessman, he acquired land: Peter Decker, 244-246, Stickney, **Squire Stickney's 1895 History of Sussex, New Jersey** , 38-40.

Intelligent and cautious, he could: Snell, **History of Sussex and Warren Counties, New Jersey,** 38. Stickney, **Squire Stickney's 1895 History of Sussex, New Jersey** , 38-39.

Sons Martinus and Joseph were: **New Jersey Archives, 1st Series,**

Vol. XXXIV, Vol 5, 1771-1780, (Trenton, NJ: MacCrellish and Quigley, 1931), 135, *Peter Decker,* 248.

But, he has also created problems: Peter Decker, 247-248.

He was born November 20, 1733: Revolutionary War Pension Application File for Martiness Decker, Service: New York File No. R7158, Transcribed by Romayne Bell Perritte, 1998, p. 1. The original family genealogy was torn from the family's Bible and sent in with Mary Decker's pension application in 1839 and still remains with the original files at NARA in Washington, D.C. A complete digital copy is available at the FDMOH

For Martinus' baptism, Pieter La Bonte: Roswell Hoes, **Baptismal and Marriage Registers of the Old Dutch Church of Kingston, Ulster County, New York (formerly named Wiltwyck and often familiarly called Esopus or 'Sopus), for One Hundred and Fifty Years from their Commencement in 1660, New York,** (Kingston, NY: De Vinne Press, 1891), 200.

Peter Gumaer, in his **History of Deerpark:** *History of Deerpark,* 75-76, *Old Deerpark Days,* Reformed Dutch Church of Deerpark, 3.

A third writer, Professor John Dolph: Tablet on Old Stone House: Impressive Unveiling Ceremonies at Germantown, Port Jervis Union, May 16, 1908, Port Jervis, NY, 1.

While no additional genealogical data: To prove that there are two different Martinus Deckers see Roswell Hoes, **Baptismal and Marriage Registers of the Old Dutch Church of Kingston, Ulster County, New York (formerly named Wiltwyck and often familiarly called Esopus or 'Sopus), for One Hundred and Fifty Years from their Commencement in 1660, New York,** 200 and 227.

Other writers have continued: Typical of the errors are those found cited here. C. G. Hine, **The Old Mine Road,** (Rahway, NJ: Rutgers University Press, Quinn Boden Co., 1963), 126-127.

Church records show Martinus: William J. Coulter, **Minisink and Wallkill Precinct Historical Chronicles, 1940-1962,** No. 147, 579. MVHS and FDMOHC.

Her parents were Johannes Dirck Westbrook: **Revolutionary War Pension Application File for Martiness Decker, Service: New York File No. R7158,** Transcribed by Romayne Bell Perritte, 1998, 1.

They were married on August 27, 1768: Decker, **The Decker Genealogy: Some Descendants of the Dutch Immigrants, Johannes Gerretsen (Decker) and Jan Broersen (Decker),** 121.

Neither Martinus nor Peter's family had slaves: Department of Commerce and Labor, Bureau of The Census, **Head of Families At The First Census Of The United States Taken In The Year 1790: New York,** (Washington:Government Printing Office, 1908), 144.

One of the most interesting things: **Revolutionary War Pension Application File for Martiness Decker, Service: New York File No. R7158,** Transcribed by Romayne Bell Perritte, 1998, 38.

A friend wrote upon his passing: **Revolutionary War Pension Application File for Martiness Decker, Service: New York File No. R7158,** Transcribed by Romayne Bell Perritte, 1998, 38.

According to a 1969 MVHS newsletter: Decker Fort Edition, 2. Royden Woodward Vosburgh, *Mahackamack Gravestone*

Inscriptions, Port Jervis, Orange County, New York, New York Genealogical and Biographical Record, Vol. XLIV, October 1913, No. 4, (New York: NY Genealogical and Biographical Society), 382.

The earliest citation for the Caskey: Genealogical Exchange, Caskey family listing, The New York Genealogical and Biographical Record, Vol 106, No. 3, July 1975, (New York: NY Genealogical and Biographical Society).

A GENERATION OF SUFFERING:
THE FRENCH AND INDIAN WAR AND THE WAR FOR
INDEPENDENCE

George Fluhr, the Pike County: George Fluhr, *A Generation of Suffering on The Upper Delaware Frontier 1742 to 1782,* 1976, Reprint from the News-Eagle, Hawley, Pa.FDMOHC

It is also not known if any: Decker Fort Edition, 2. In this newsletter the author states that Decker was a lieutenant in both the French and Indian and Revolutionary War but no source is given to check.

No information survives that describes: Alan and Barbara Aimone, *Pre-Revolution Fortified Places of New York,* Journal of the Council of Abandoned Military Posts, Vol IX, No. 4, No. 34, Winter, 1977-78, Periodical, 35.

During the French and Indian War: Eager, **An Outline History of Orange County, Newburgh**, 381-382, **History of Deerpark in Orange County,** 56-57.

Another difficult period for these: For more information see Osborne, Peter, *The New York-New Jersey Boundary Line: While New Jersey Dozed, New York Was Wide Awake,* (Port Jervis, NY:

Minisink Valley Historical Society, 1992).

Peter Decker's name appears: Plot or Description of the Lands Formerly Granted to Captain John Evans, the land granted to Matthew Ling and others Commonly Called Minisink Patent, 1765, Map. no. 440, New York State Office of General Services, Albany, New York, *Peter Decker,* 244.

Through these years Peter Decker: Peter Decker, p 246.

Decker offered no assistance: Peter Decker, 246, Stickney, **Squire Stickney's 1895 History of Sussex, New Jersey** 38.

Decker would also be arrested: Peter Decker, 246-7.

Tax collectors and militia commanders: For more information on the dimensions of the dispute and maps see Osborne, **The New York-New Jersey Boundary Line: While New Jersey Dozed, New York Was Wide Awake.**

John Adams, a major figure: **John Adams,** David McCullough, (New York: Simon and Schuster, , 2001), 78.

It is believed that most: Forts Once Dotted Tri-State Region, Calvin Van Etten Crane, undated newspaper article with no source given, FDMOHC, **History of Deerpark,** 89.

It is described as a wooden: Fort Decker: Minisink Valley Historical Society, compiled by C. Richard Carey, c. 1982, p. 5, FDMOHC.

In addition, there were: Pre-Revolution Fortified Places of New York, Alan and Barbara Aimone, Journal of the Council of Abandoned Military Posts, Vol IX, No. 3, No. 33, Fall, 1977, Periodical, 17. There is no citation in this article to indicate where this data came from.

Major Johannes Decker's fortified house: Stickney, **Squire Stickney's 1895 History of Sussex, New Jersey,** 17.

One of the challenges for the commanders: Pre-Revolution Fortified Places of New York, Alan and Barbara Aimone, Journal of the Council of Abandoned Military Posts, Vol IX, No. 3, No. 33, Fall, 1977, Periodical, 17.

As historian Mildred Parker Seese: Mildred Parker Seese,**Old Orange Houses, Vol II,** (Middletown, New York, Book Mill Volume, 1943), 21.

When Joseph Brant, who played: Vernon Leslie, **The Battle of Minisink: A Revolutionary War Engagement in the Upper Delaware Valley,** 2nd edition, (Middletown, NY: T. Emmett Henderson, 1976), 117.

The pension application of Martin Cuykendall: Martin Cuykendall Pension Application, Revolutionary War Pension Record S-12649, New York, NARA, North Carolina State Library (Raleigh), Series M804, Roll #727.

The most significant description of what: Benjamin Davis Pension Application, Revolutionary War Pension Record S-23187, New York, NARA, North Carolina State Library (Raleigh), Series M804, Roll #750.

A third applicant, James Burt: James Burt Pension Application, Revolutionary War Pension Record S-12388, New York, NARA, North Carolina State Library (Raleigh), Series M804, Roll #429.

William Knapp, another militia man: William Knapp Pension Application, Revolutionary War Pension Record S-6015, New York, NARA, North Carolina State Library (Raleigh), Series M804, Roll #1500.

Richard Clark describes part: Richard Clark Pension Application, Revolutionary War Pension Record S-12509, New York, NARA, North Carolina State Library (Raleigh), Series M804, Roll #564.

Moses Knapp, stationed at the Fort: Moses Knapp Pension

Application, Revolutionary War Pension Record S-13675, New York, NARA, North Carolina State Library (Raleigh), Series M804, Roll #1500.

A much later description: Decker Fort Edition, 2. This same article says that Hayne and his wife, after hearing about the raid and its progress, fled the fort and went to New Jersey. This statement contradicts other sources however.

Another question concerns the disposition: "The Old Stone House: Germantown's Historic Building", The Port Jervis Union, Port Jervis, New York, May 26, 1893, 1. The author of the newspaper article credits Rev. Dr. Samuel Mills with much of the information in this article. He was the pastor of the Dutch Reformed Church of Deerpark from 1857-1871 and President of the Minisink Valley Historical Society from1889-1902.

These were similar to stumps: Ibid.

Sickness was easily passed: Pre-Revolution Fortified Places of New York, Alan and Barbara Aimone, Journal of the Council of Abandoned Military Posts, Vol IX, No. 3, No. 33, Fall, 1977, Periodical, 8.

Both Martinus Decker and Martin Decker: Eager, **An Outline History of Orange County**, 420. The Martinus Decker Jr. listed is probably the second of the Martinus Decker's mentioned earlier. It was Dutch tradition to add junior after a male's name if there was an older person by the same name even though they were not father and son.

These men also served in the Orange County: James, Roberts, **New York in the Revolution As Colony and State**, 2nd edition, (Albany, NY: Brandow Printing Co., 1898), 191

He would have also been familiar: Roberts, **New York in the**

Revolution As Colony and State, 191 and 255.

Another interesting connection: **Public Papers of George Clinton: First Governor of New York 1777-1795 1801-1804, Volume III,** (Albany, NY: James Lyon, New York State Printer, 1900), 717-720.

After their capture, Decker attended: There is some dispute as to this date, Robert Land's biographer believes that it occurred in 1779 and this is also confirmed by the court martial's proceeding that can be found in George Washington's papers. However Decker's pension application says it happened in 1781. However, both accounts do agree on the details of what happened. Elliott, James, **If Ponies Rode Men: The Journey of Robert Land, 1777-1791,** (Stoney Creek, Ontario: Barrie Press, 1999), 221-222. Revolutionary War Pension Application File for Martiness Decker, Service: New York File No. R7158, Transcribed by Romayne Bell Perritte, 1998, p. 1. George Washington Papers, Series 4, Reel 56, February 10, 1779-March 25, 1779, Library of Congress, Washington, D.C.

After his death and upon the application of Martinus: Revolutionary War Pension Application File for Martiness Decker, Service: New York File No. R7158, Transcribed by Romayne Bell Perritte, 1998, 14 and 17.

A Martin Decker is also listed: Roberts, **New York in the Revolution As Colony and State**, 255.

Peter Gumaer wrote that Decker was: Revolutionary War Pension Application File for Martiness Decker, Service: New York File No. R7158, Transcribed by Romayne Bell Perritte, 1998.

Gumaer also wrote that Decker: Ibid.

Peter Van Auken later testified: Ibid.

Wilhelmus Westfall's service in the American Revolution: Wilhelmus Westfall Pension Application, Revolutionary War Pension Record S-15322, New York, NARA, North Carolina State Library (Raleigh) Series M-804, Roll # 2538

The full transcription of Martinus Decker's: Revolutionary War Pension Application File for Martiness Decker, Service: New York File No. R7158, Transcribed by Romayne Bell Perritte, 1998, 38.

JOSEPH BRANT'S RAIDS OF 1778 AND 1779

Several members of the pioneer families: The 200th Anniversary of the Defense of the Peenpack Area October 13, 1778, Compiled by C. Richard Carey, Published by the Town of Deerpark Bicentennial Commission, 1978. Snell, **History of Sussex and Warren Counties, New Jersey,** 55.

That she has a distinct recollection: Revolutionary War Pension Application File for Martiness Decker, Service: New York File No. R7158, Transcribed by Romayne Bell Perritte, 1998, 38.

Peter Van Auken a resident: Ibid.

That on the nineteenth day of July 1779 long: Wilhelmus Westfall Pension Application, Revolutionary War Pension Record S-15322, New York, NARA, North Carolina State Library (Raleigh) Series M-804, Roll # 2538

That in 1779 when the: Wilhelmus Westfall Pension Application, Revolutionary War Pension Record S-15322, New York, NARA, North Carolina State Library (Raleigh) Series M-804, Roll # 2538

At least one account says: Lytell, Herman, *Old Canal Landmarks: The Old Stone Fort, The Delaware and Hudson Canal: Material For A*

History of Port Jervis, Prepared for the Local History Project of the Works Progress Administration for the Port Jervis Free Library. 1935-1937, 443, FDMOHC.

Joseph Brant in his report: Leslie, **The Battle of Minisink: A Revolutionary War Engagement in the Upper Delaware Valley,** 117.

Ker reported the loss of fifty: Ibid., 133-134.

Militia leader Colonel John Hathorn: Ibid. 128.

Governor Clinton would later write: **Public Papers of George Clinton: First Governor of New York 1777-1795 1801-1804, Volume III,** 165.

A party of two hundred and forty people traveled: Leslie,**The Battle of Minisink: A Revolutionary War Engagement in the Upper Delaware Valley,** 134.

At the time of Brant's second raid: Museum Matters, 1, A Bit Of Local History, 5.

It is also believed the families: **History of Deerpark,** 91.

No doubt the families living: Ibid., 90.

At least one nineteenth century newspaper: Leslie, **The Battle of Minisink: A Revolutionary War Engagement in the Upper Delaware Valley,** 225.

There is no evidence to confirm: Ibid.

One final story that has passed down: Stickney, **Squire Stickney's 1895 History of Sussex, New Jersey,** 34.

The ceremony was conducted: Decker Fort Edition, 2-3.

A wedding was said to have followed in 1780: Lytell, Herman, *Old Canal Landmarks: The Old Stone Fort, The Delaware and Hudson Canal: Material For A History of Port Jervis,* Prepared for the Local History Project of the Works Progress Administration for the

Port Jervis Free Library. 1935-1937, 443, FDMOHC, *Decker Fort Edition*, 2-3. William J. Coulter in a *Wantage Recorder* article of November 9, 1934 believes that the marriage occurred in June 1778. The first issue by this marriage was Cathrina who was baptized in either September or October of 1780 making the 1778 previously cited or the 1780 date conceivable.

Another Westfall tradition is that: "*The Old Stone House: Germantown's Historic Building*", The Port Jervis Union, Port Jervis, New York, May 26, 1893, 3, *Museum Matters*, 1, *A Bit Of Local History*, 5.

In 1777 Indians slaughtered: Snell, **History of Sussex and Warren Counties, New Jersey,** 54-55.

THE REBUILDING OF FORT DECKER

Nathan Ker, the Goshen minister: Leslie, **The Battle of Minisink: A Revolutionary War Engagement in the Upper Delaware Valley,** 134.

A fire expert concluded after: Conversation with Leo Fleming, Port Jervis Fire Inspector, September 1, 1988.

The foundations were found to: A Bit Of Local History, 5.

Another history of the building written: Old Deerpark Days, Reformed Dutch Church of Deerpark, 3. The author of the 1902 Church Life article may have relied upon the 1887 newspaper article for some of his material as some of the quotations are almost identical or may have in fact been the same person.

A 1903 article states that: A Relic of Pioneer Days: A Romance of the Old Stone House in Germantown, The Port Jervis Gazette, Port Jervis, New York, February 16, 1903, 1.

The only author to suggest that: Negro Slave Defended Mistress in Stone Fort, Middletown Daily Time-Press, Middletown, New York,

October 17, 1925, 1.

In his seminal work: History of Deerpark, 143.

One author believes that: A Bit Of Local History, 5.

One source says that only: Nails 110 Years Old, Port Jervis Union, Port Jervis, New York, June 24, 1903, not paginated. FDMOHC *Large stones were interlocked: Built To Last: New York State's Extraordinary Stone Houses Are Monuments To Dutch and Huguenot Craftsmanship,* Michael Hurewitz, Historic Preservation, July/August 1986, National Historic Trust, Washington, DC, 50.

To give some perspective of how: Ibid.

It usually took about four: Ibid.., 51.

Masons and carpenters were often hired to: Another explanation comes from the article entitled *"Tablet on Old Stone House,"* Port Jervis Union, May 16, 1908, Port Jervis, New York, p. 1. In this case the author argues that the second MD is for Martinus Decker's grandson. Because so much of the article's history is suspect, this assertion may also be incorrect.

There is a formal or parlor room: Built To Last: New York State's Extraordinary Stone Houses Are Monuments To Dutch and Huguenot Craftsmanship, Michael Hurewitz, Historic Preservation, July/August 1986, National Historic Trust, Washington, DC, 51.

The original walls were plastered: Ibid., 51.

This author, however, questions: Roy Vail to Cornelius Cuddeback, President, Minisink Valley Historical Society, undated, FDMO-HC.

Most of the second floor's 1793: Roy Vail believed that the upstairs doors had actually been downstairs and moved to the second floor at a later date. Roy Vail to Cornelius Cuddeback, President, Minisink Valley Historical Society, undated, FDMOHC. Note from Robert Aber, January 17, 2007

Vail believed the ceiling boards: Roy Vail to Cornelius Cuddeback, President, Minisink Valley Historical Society, undated, FDMO-HC. *Museum Matters,* 1.

As Harrison Meeske said in: Harrison Meeske, **The Hudson Valley Dutch and Their Houses,** (Walden, NY: Purple Mountain Press, 2003), 127.

That is something we tend: Built To Last: New York State's Extraordinary Stone Houses Are Monuments To Dutch and Huguenot Craftsmanship, Michael Hurewitz, Historic Preservation, July/August 1986, National Historic Trust, Washington, DC, 53.

THE DECKER FARM

It has been suggested, although: Museum Matters, 1. *Decker Fort Edition,* 3.

Because of the confusion surrounding: Stickney, **Squire Stickney's 1895 History of Sussex, New Jersey,** 8.

Another author thought Jan Decker: Decker, **The Decker Genealogy: Some Descendants of the Dutch Immigrants, Johannes Gerretsen (Decker) and Jan Broersen (Decker),** 121.

This is of particular interest because: **James McCoy's Abstract of Sussex County Deeds, East Jersey Deeds, Amboy S-4,** 73.

The deed is from Martinus: Martinus and Mary Decker to Martinus Decker Jr., Deed dated September 15, 1798, FDMOHC

An assessment roll in 1775 shows: Edward Ruttenber and Lewis Clark, **History of Orange County, New York,** (Philadelphia:

Everts and Peck, 1881), 704. The junior Decker is probably, as mentioned earlier, a relative by the same name but from a different family.

Martinus' son, Peter, did have: Department of Commerce and Labor, Bureau of The Census, **Head of Families At The First Census Of The United States Taken In The Year 1790: New York,** (Washington:Government Printing Office, 1908), 144.

There were 370 heads of families: Ibid.., 10.

Out of the forty-nine homes: C. Richard Carey, **1798 Assessment Records, Town of Deerpark, Deerpark, New York,** c. 1983.

This made the total value: C. Richard Carey, **1798 Assessment Records, Town of Deerpark, Deerpark, New York,** c. 1983. C. Richard Carey to Peter Osborne, Notes on Martinus Decker in the 1798 Federal Assessment for the Town of Minisink, undated, FDMOHC.

The executors of his will were: Old Deerpark Days, Reformed Dutch Church of Deerpark, 3.

Decker was active in Town of Minisink: Ruttenber and Clark, **History of Orange County, New York,** 663.

Richard Decker sold the stone house: Richard Decker to John Kent, Deed numbered R-77-1815, Orange County Government Center, Goshen, New York, FDMOHC.

At least one account states: A Bit Of Local History, 6.

THE ST. JOHN HOTEL

His business career was interrupted: Obituary, Stephen St. John, September 8, 1870, Family Gazette, Port Jervis, New York, unpaginated. FDMOHC.

It was during this time: John Kent to Stephen St. John and Benjamin Dodge, Deed numbered U-37-1819, Orange County Government Center, Goshen, New York, FDMOHC

Soon they moved their business: Obituary, Stephen St. John, September 8, 1870, Family Gazette, Port Jervis, New York, unpaginated, FDMOHC.

Philenda married George Malven: Obituary, Stephen St. John, September 8, 1870, Family Gazette, Port Jervis, New York, unpaginated. FDMOHC. Stephen St. John Family Genealogy and Burial Locations, compiled by Nancy Conod, January 15, 2006.

Stephen St. John, an astute businessman: A Bit Of Local History, 6.

Lord, Jervis and St. John carried on: John B. Jervis, **The Reminiscences of John B. Jervis: Engineer of the Old Croton,** forward by Robert Vogel. edited with introduction by Neal Fitzsimons. (Syracuse, New York: Syracuse University Press, 1971), 72

The kitchen may have also been: Roy Vail to Cornelius Cuddeback, President, Minisink Valley Historical Society, undated, FDMOHC, Donald Carpentier to Richard Tarbell, January 16, 1980, FDMOHC.

The paneled fireplace in the former: Roy Vail to Cornelius Cuddeback, President, Minisink Valley Historical Society, FDMOHC, undated.

It may have been during this time: Decker Fort Edition, 4.

Stephen and Abigal St. John lived: A Bit Of Local History, 6.

St. John was a plain, temperate: Obituary, Stephen St. John, September 8, 1870, Family Gazette, Port Jervis, New York, unpaginated. FDMOHC.

Abigal had also been buried: Death of Mrs. Stephen St. John, The
Family Gazette, Port Jervis, New York, April 26, 1870, unpaginated, FDMOHC.

His family purchased a large: **Report on the Proposed Use of an
Abandoned Burial Ground for the Erection of A School
House at Port Jervis,** New York State Board of Health,
Extracted from Fifth Annual Report, 1884, Don Gumaer and
Nancy Bello, **The Records Of The Laurel Grove Cemetery,
Port Jervis, New York,** (Port Jervis, NY: Minisink Valley
Historical Society, 2000), 33.

In a late nineteenth century newspaper: A Bit Of Local History, 3.

The Adirondack-styled structure could: Ron Dupont and Kevin
Wright, **High Point of the Blue Mountains,** (Newton, NJ:
Sussex County Historical Society, 1990), 18-21.

Entertaining guests ran in the family. Ibid.

THE DECKER STONE HOUSE IN THE NINETEENTH CENTURY

An interesting citation can be: **US Federal Census Records,** New
York, Orange County, Port Jervis, 1880.

However, with few records available: A Bit Of Local History, 3. This
article says that Youmans bought the property and lived in it, but
the property records do not agree. It may be that Youmans rented the property with an option to buy it, and then defaulted
because there are no deeds for this property in his name. The
1893 newspaper history of the Fort also says that the ownership
had passed through several hands. *"The Old Stone House:
Germantown's Historic Building",* The Port Jervis Union, Port Jervis,
New York, May 26, 1893, 1.

This contract must have been extended: Executors of the Estate of

Stephen St. John to John Cannon, Sr, Deed numbered 243-395-1872, Orange County Government Center, Goshen, New York.
They had embarked in Liverpool: Ancestry.com, New York Passenger Lists Record, July 1, 2006.

Of Rose, we know almost: Compilation of city directory data on Cannon family by Nancy Vocci, compilation of Federal Census data on Cannon family by Nancy Conod, FDMOHC

In the 1874 City Directory he: Compilation of city directory data on Cannon family by Nancy Vocci, FDMOHC.

He had retired from the Erie: Obituary, John Cannon, Port Jervis Union, Port Jervis, New York, March 19, 1915, 1, Orange County Coroner's Report, 1916, (Goshen, NY: Orange County)

He committed suicide almost one: Orange County Coroner's Report, 1916, (Goshen, NY: Orange County) *Obituary, John Cannon,* Port Jervis Union, March 10, 1916, 2.

His wife Mary had died March 18, 1915: Obituary, Mary Cannon, Port Jervis Union, Port Jervis, New York, March 10, 1916, 1.

Also living there at the time: Compilation of city directory data on Cannon family by Nancy Vocci, compilation of Federal Census data on Cannon family by Nancy Conod, FDMOHC

Nell was a clerk at the: Obituary, Nellie Cannon, Port Jervis Union Gazette, Port Jervis, New York, September 7, 1965.

It was later demolished because of: All of the deeds and associated paperwork that transfer the properties of the Fort Decker Compound are located in the FDMOHC.

On April 27, 1970, acting in her role: Will of Nellie R. Cannon, File No. 826-65, Orange County Surrogate's Court, Goshen, New York, September 5, 1965.

THE DECKER STONE HOUSE IN THE 20TH CENTURY

For more than fifty years: Deaths and Funerals: "Mrs. Sarah M. Campfield," December 16, 1956, Port Jervis Union Gazette, Port Jervis, New York, 1.

Her obituary said she was well-liked: Deaths and Funerals: Ibid.

He is often remembered for: "Death and Funerals: C. Mose Campfield," June 1, 1971, Port Jervis Union Gazette, Port Jervis, New York.

From a previous marriage there: "Obituary: Mrs. Moses Campfield," February 7, 1975, Port Jervis Union Gazette, Port Jervis, New York.

Coslick went over to the coffin: Interview with Bud Coslick by the author, 1980s.

All of the deceased family members: Don Gumaer and Nancy Bello, **The Records Of The Laurel Grove Cemetery, Port Jervis, New York,** (Port Jervis, NY: Minisink Valley Historical Society, 2000), 33.

In June, 1903, the original 1793 roof: "Nails 110 Years Old," Port Jervis Union, Port Jervis, New York, June 24, 1903, 1.

It fell over, for reasons still unknown: Interviews with Flojean Collette, 1990-2004.

As the weapon was discharged: "Accidental Shooting: Stanley Canfield Wounded In Neck By A Boy Companion," August 17, 1903, Port Jervis Union, Port Jervis, New York, 1.

A second story appeared on: "Little Stanley Campfield Succumbs to His Injuries," Port Jervis Union, Port Jervis, New York, September 29, 1903, 1.

Finally, it has been suggested: Interviews with Jacob Hornbeck, 1980s.

His obituary is sad to read: "Little Stanley Campfield Succumbs to His

Injuries," Port Jervis Union, Port Jervis, New York, September 29, 1903, 1.

The tragedy was an enormous one: Interviews with Jacob Hornbeck, 1980s.

In the process of cleaning: Informal Interview with Mrs. Jeffrey Auerbach, c. 1990

Family members believe that: Interviews with Flojean Collette, 1990-2004. John Mallalieu to Peter Osborne, July 20, 2005.

He did not think it: Interviews with Jacob Hornbeck, 1980s.

Her mother told her to never: "What's Buried in the Basement of Fort Decker," TheGazette, Port Jervis, New York October 27, 1995, 1, Interviews with Flojean Collette, 1990-2004.

The fire spread slowly and crept: "Decker Fort, or Stone House, Built in 1793, Saved by Firemen", The Port Jervis Gazette, Port Jervis, New York, January 22, 1924, 3.

The reporter also noted the Winters: Ibid.

FORT DECKER AS A MUSEUM

He was also the President: "The Old Stone House: Germantown's Historic Building", The Port Jervis Union, Port Jervis, New York, May 26, 1893.

Two of the more interesting attendees: "Tablet on Old Stone House: Impressive Unveiling Ceremonies at Germantown," Port Jervis Union, May 16, 1908, Port Jervis, New York. Mrs. Mills husband, Samuel W. Mills provided material for a history of the stone house in an 1893 newspaper article.

Another tradition has it that she wanted: Handwritten notes by Cornelius Cuddeback, a former president of the Society, undated, FDMOHC.

On October 2, 1937, Mrs. Frederick W. Best: Peter Osborne, **The Historic Markers of the City of Port Jervis and the Town of Deerpark, New York,** (Port Jervis, NY: Minisink Valley Historical Society, 1989), 2002.

It was not until after 1960 that: Interviews with Flojean Collette, 1990-2004.

In 1966, discussion about purchasing: "Port Asked to Consider Museum at Decker's Fort," December 10, 1966, Port Jervis Union Gazette, Port Jervis, New York, unpaginated, FDMOHC.

At a special meeting of the directors: Decker Fort Edition, 4.

Within a week an offer was: Gertrude L. Kellam, administratrix of the Estate of Lauretta Lyons, James Lyons and Raymond Lyons to the Minisink Valley Historical Society, Liber 1846, p. 487, Orange County Government Center, Goshen, New York.

The acquisition was made with the proceeds: An MVHS February 1973 financial report states that the real estate and house was valued at $3,532.

A ceremony was held to commemorate: "Historical Society Accepts Keys to Fort," Union Gazette, Port Jervis, New York, May 27, 1970, unpaginated.

There was much interest in the larger: Museum Matters, 1.

The building was nominated for: "Port's Oldest Building On National Register," July 23, 1974, Port Jervis Union Gazette, Port Jervis, New York, unpaginated, FDMOHC.

The author has concluded that: Museum Matters, 1.

One of his recommendations was: Roy Vail to Cornelius Cuddeback, President, Minisink Valley Historical Society, undated, FDMOHC.

Ultimately, the Society's board did: Correspondence files, MVHS,

FDMOHC.

A floor covering, perhaps green linoleum: "*Old Stone House Revisited,*" October 2, 1972, Port Jervis Union Gazette, Port Jervis, New York, 3.

Wallboard was removed from the: "*Old Stone House Revisited,*" October 2, 1972, Port Jervis Union Gazette, Port Jervis, New York, 3.

The stove was then probably placed: Ibid.

It was determined that it would: William and Linda McCann to the Minisink Valley Historical Society, Liber 2176, 913, Orange County Government Center, Goshen, New York.

On December 7,1981, the society purchased: Gabriel DiGiantamasco to Minisink Valley Historical Society, Liber 2212, 300 and Betty Kranz to Minisink Valley Historical Society, Liber 2809, 274, Orange County Government Center, Goshen, New York.

He also provided the Society with: Donald Carpentier to Richard Tarbell, Vice President, Minisink Valley Historical Society, January 16, 1980, FDMOHC.

WHO TURNS ON THE LIGHTS AT 9:15?

Neither told the other about what they: Interviews with Doris Hammond, 1990s.

Those items were checked and: Linda Zimmerman, **Haunted Hudson Valley III,** (Blooming Grove, NY: A Spirited Books Publication, 2001), 4-5.

Finally, she believes that there is no such: Linda Zimmerman, **Haunted Hudson Valley III,** (Blooming Grove, NY: A Spirited Books Publication, 2001), 5-6.

At the moment the photographer took: Ibid.

Infrared footage was later analyzed, and: Ibid.

At some undetermined time she moved: Nancy Bello to Alan White, July 2, 2001, FDMOHC.

At one point the owner, Betty Kranz: Interviews with Betty Kranz, 1980s.

VIGILANCE AND PERSEVERANCE

In 1887 a newspaper reporter wrote: A Bit Of Local History, 3.

BIBLIOGRAPHIC ESSAY

The author's entire collection of notes, letters and photocopies and various records generated by this project were placed in the Fort Decker Museum of History Collection (FDMOHC) at Fort Decker. It is believed that most, if not all of the articles ever written about Fort Decker are included in this bibliography. Copies of all of the materials found in the endnotes can be found in the Society's archives or FDMOHC.

As much as we know about the Society's stone house museum, there are still many things that we do not know about the building. Some of these include a lack of knowledge about the Hayne, Decker and Westfall families and the building's history during the nineteenth century. The records of the property transactions prior to 1798 cannot be found which would clear up much of the mystery of the building's eighteenth century history.

The earliest histories of the building that were written relied heavily on just three late nineteenth century newspaper articles which were passing down traditions that the writers had heard. However, they are, except for the Revolutionary War pension applications, the closest to contemporary accounts that can be found. The author attempted to check all of the materials that were not readily available to those authors, and of course, the materials that have been created since the writing of those articles.

BIBLIOGRAPHY

BOOKS

Angell, Pauline. **Fifty Years on the Frontier With The Dutch Congregation at Maghaghkamik.** Port Jervis, NY: Reformed Dutch Church of Deerpark, 1937.

Anjou, Gustave. **Ulster County, NY, Probate Records, Vol. 1.** New York: Privately published, 1906.

Carey, C. Richard. **1798 Assessment Records, Town of Deerpark.** Deerpark, NY: Town Historian, 1983.

____. **Fort Decker, Minisink Valley Historical Society.** Deerpark, NY: Town Historian, c. 1982.

____. **The 200th Anniversary of the Defense of the Peenpack Area October 13, 1778.** Deerpark, NY: Town of Deerpark Bicentennial Commission, 1978.

Clark, Lewis and Edward Ruttenber, **History of Orange County, New York.** Philadelphia: Everts and Peck, 1881.

Cuddeback, William L. **Caudebec in America.** Port Jervis, NY: Minisink Valley Historical Society, 1999.

Decker, Benton Weaver. **The Decker Genealogy: Some Descendants of the Dutch Immigrants, Johannes (Decker)**

and Jan Broersen (Decker). San Diego, California: Budget Book Manufacturing Co., 1980.

Delaware and Hudson Company: A Century of Progress. Albany, New York: Delaware and Hudson Company, 1923.

Dupont, Ron and Kevin Wright, **High Point of the Blue Mountains.** Newton, NJ: Sussex County Historical Society, 1990.

Dutch Church Records of the Machakemeck and Mennisenk Churches. Port Jervis, NY: Deerpark Reformed Church, 1899.

Dutch-English and English-Dutch Dictionary. New York:Van Riemsdyck Book Service, 1945.

Eager, Samuel. **An Outline History of Orange County.** Newburgh, NY: S.T. Callahan, 1846-7.

Elliott, James. **If Ponies Rode Men: The Journey of Robert Land, 1777-1791.** Stoney Creek, Ontario: Barrie Press, 1999.

Ferling, John. **Setting the World Ablaze: Washington, Adams, Jefferson and the American Revolution.** New York: Oxford University Press, 2000.

Fluhr, George. **A Generation of Suffering on The Upper Delaware Frontier 1742 to 1782.** Reprint from the News-Eagle, Hawley, Pa., 1976.

Gumaer, Donald and Nancy Bello. **The Laurel Grove Cemetery Records, Port Jervis, New York 1857-2003.** Port Jervis, NY: Minisink Valley Historical Society, 1999.

Gumaer, Peter E., **A History of Deerpark in Orange County.** Port Jervis, New York: Minisink Valley Historical Society and Port Jervis Union Print, 1890.

Hardyston Memorial, A History of the Township and The

North Presbyterian Church, Hardyston, Sussex County, New Jersey. Newton, New Jersey: New Jersey Herald Print, 1888.

Head of Families At The First Census Of The United States Taken In The Year 1790: New York. Department of Commerce and Labor, Bureau of The Census. Washington, D.C.: Government Printing Office, 1908.

Hine, C. G. **The Old Mine Road.** Rahway, New Jersey: Rutgers University Press and Quinn Boden Co., 1963.

Hoes, Roswell. **Baptismal and Marriage Registers of the Old Dutch Church of Kingston, Ulster County, New York (formerly named Wiltwyck and often familiarly called Esopus or 'Sopus), for One Hundred and Fifty Years from their Commencement in 1660.** New York: De Vinne Press, 1891.

Hutchinson, Elmer. **Documents Relating To The Colonial, Revolutionary and Post-Revolutionary History of the State of New Jersey, 1st Series, Vol. XL, 1806-1809.** Trenton, New Jersey: MacCrellish and Quigley, 1947.

Inners, Jon and Peter Osborne, **Blood and Mayhem on The Delaware: Historical Geography of Brant's Minisink Raid and the Battle of Minisink - July 1779.** Harrisburg, Pennsylvania: Pennsylvania Geological Survey, 2001.

Jervis, John B.. **The Reminiscences of John B. Jervis: Engineer of the Old Croton.** Forward by Robert Vogel. Edited with introduction by Neal Fitzsimons. Syracuse, New York: Syracuse University Press, 1971.

Johnston, John W, **Reminiscences.** Port Jervis, New York: Minisink Valley Historical Society, 1987.

Kraft, Herbert. **The Dutch, The Indians and the Quest for Copper: Pahaquarry and the Old Mine Road.** Orange, New Jersey: Seton Hall University, 1996.

Leslie, Vernon.**The Battle of Minisink: A Revolutionary War Engagement in the Upper Delaware Valley,** 2nd edition. Middletown, New York: T. Emmett Henderson, 1976.

Lord, Philip. **Documenting Prehistoric Habitation in Your Community: A Guide For Local Historians.** New York State Museum, Circular No. 55, Albany, New York: The University of the State of New York, New York State Museum, 1980.

Lowenthal, Larry. **From the Coal Fields to the Hudson.** Walton, New York: Purple Mountain Press, 1997.

Lyon, James. **Public Papers of George Clinton: First Governor of New York 1777-1795 1801-1804, Volume III,** New York State Printer, 1900.

Lytell, Herman. *Old Canal Landmarks: The Old Stone Fort, The Delaware and Hudson Canal: Material For A History of Port Jervis,* Prepared for the Local History Project of the Work Progress Administration. Unpublished manuscript. 1935-1937.

McCullough, David. **John Adams.** New York: Simon and Schuster, 2001.

Meeske, Harrison. **The Hudson Valley Dutch and Their Houses.** Walden, New York: Purple Mountain Press, 2003.

New Jersey Archives, 1st Series, Vol. XXXIV, Vol 5, 1771-1780. Trenton, NJ: MacCrellish and Quiley, 1931.

Ogden,Lucile Gumaer.**The Journal of the Records of Peter Gumaer 1771-1869.** Middletown, New York: The Service Press, 1983.

Osborne, Peter. **The Port Jervis Area Heritage Commission**

Salutes the Decker Stone House 1793-1993. Port Jervis, New York: Port Jervis Heritage Commission, 1993.

_____ . The Port Jervis Area Heritage Commission Remembers the New York-New Jersey Border War. Port Jervis, New York: Port Jervis Area Heritage Commission, 1992.

_____ . The Port Jervis Area Heritage Commission Salutes the Port Jervis Trolley System. Port Jervis, New York: Port Jervis Area Heritage Commission, 1990.

_____ .The Port Jervis Area Heritage Commission Salutes the Gilded Age. Port Jervis, New York: Port Jervis Area Heritage Commission, 1991.

_____ . Graveyard Art and its History. Port Jervis, New York: Port Jervis Area Heritage Commission, 1995.

_____ . The Chartering of the City of Port Jervis: 1907-1997. Port Jervis, New York: Port Jervis Area Heritage Commission, 1997.

_____ . The Historic Markers of the City of Port Jervis and the Town of Deerpark, New York. Port Jervis, New York: Minisink Valley Historical Society, 2002.

_____ . A Salute to Samuel B. Farnum. Port Jervis, New York: Port Jervis Area Heritage Commission, 1989.

Perritte, Romayne B. Revolutionary War Pension Application File for Martiness Decker, Service: New York File No. R7158. privately published, 1998.

_____ . The Family of Martin Decker and Hulday Kuykendall, privately published, 1995.

Reynolds, Helen. Dutch Houses In The Hudson Valley Before 1776. New York: Dover Press, 1965.

Report on the Proposed Use of an Abandoned Burial

Ground for the Erection of A School House at Port Jervis. New York State Board of Health, Albany, New York, extracted from Fifth Annual Report, 1884.

Roberts, James. **New York in the Revolution As Colony and State,** Albany, New York: Brandow Printing Co., 1898.

Sanderson, Dorothy. **The Delaware and Hudson Canalway: Carrying Coals to Rondout**. Ellenville, New York: Rondout Valley Publishing Company, 1974.

Seese, Mildred Parker. **Old Orange Houses (Vol.. 1).** Middletown, New York: The Whilock Press, 1941.

Seese, Mildred Parker. **Old Orange Houses, Vol II.** Middletown, New York: Book Mill Volume, 1943.

Shaughnessy, Jim. **Delaware and Hudson,** Syracuse, New York: Syracuse University Press, 1997.

Snell, James P. **History of Sussex and Warren Counties, New Jersey**. Philadelphia: Everts and Peck, 1881.

Stickney, Amelia. **That Ancient Trail: The Old Mine Road.** Trenton, New Jersey: Petty Printing Company, 1942.

Stickney, Charles. **Squire Stickney's 1895 History of Sussex, New Jersey.** Baltimore: Gateway Press, 1977.

Stickney, Charles. **History of the Minisink Region,** Port Jervis, New York: Minisink Valley Historical Society, 1867.

Sussex Borough Tercentenary Committee. **Deckertown-Sussex Tercentenary Record: A History of Borough of Sussex, NJ**, Newton, New Jersey: New Jersey Herald, 1964.

Swayze, Francis J. **Historical Address: Sesqui-Centennial Sussex County, New Jersey,** Newton, New Jersey: New Jersey Herald, 1903.

Wakefield, Manville. **Coal Boats to Tidewater,** Grahamsville,

New York: Wakefair Press, 1971.

Zimmerman, Linda, **Haunted Hudson Valley III**, Blooming Grove, New York: A Spirited Books Publication, 2001.

ARTICLES

Aimone, Alan and Barbara Aimone. *Pre-Revolution Fortified Places of New York.* Vol IX, No. 3, No. 33, Fall, 1977, No. 4, Winter 1977-1978, *Periodical,* Journal of the Council of Abandoned Military Posts.

Clyne, Patricia. *Fort Decker's Halls are Boughed With Holley.* Hudson Valley Magazine, December 1986.

Coulter, William J. *Minisink and Wallkill Precinct Historical Chronicles, 1940-1962,* MVHS and FDMOHC.

Decker Fort Edition. The Mennisienk, MVHS, September 1969.

Hurewitz, Michael. *Built To Last: New York State's Extraordinary Stone Houses Are Monuments To Dutch and Huguenot Craftsmanship.* Historic Preservation, Washington, DC, National Historic Trust, July/August 1986.

Old Deerpark Days. Church Life, Reformed Dutch Church of Deerpark , Port Jervis, New York, Vol XV, No. 8, November 1902.

Osborne, Peter. *The New York-New Jersey Boundary Line: While New Jersey Dozed, New York Was Wide Awake.* Port Jervis, New York, Minisink Valley Historical Society, 1992.

_____.*The Minisink Valley Historical Society: The First One Hundred Years.* Arden, New York, Orange County Historical Society Journal, 1989.

_____.*The Old Decker Stone House.* Port Jervis, New York, Port Jervis Diamond Jubilee, Port Jervis Area Heritage Commission,

1982.

_____ . *Russel Farnum Lord: Chief Engineer of the Delaware and Hudson Canal.* Arden, New York, Orange County Historical Society Journal, 1983.

Port Jervis Historians Acquire Fort Decker. Museum Matters, Goshen, New York, Orange County Community of Museums and Galleries, Vol. IV, No. 3, July-September 1970.

Remembering Lt. Martinus Decker: Perseverance and Vigilance During the War For Independence. Observer, Sullivan County Historical Society, Hurleyville, New York, Vol. 22, Issue 5, September-October 2002.

Strasser, Theresa Coyne, *Peter Decker (ca. 1711-1773) of Sussex County, New Jersey, and Some of His Descendants.* National Genealogical Quarterly, Vol. 72, No. 4, December 1984.

The Oldest House in Port Jervis. Olde Ulster, Ulster County Historical Society, Vol. VI, No. 11.

Vosburgh, Royden Woodward, *Mahackamack Gravestone Inscriptions, Port Jervis, Orange County, New York.* New York Genealogical and Biographical Record, Vol. XLIV, October 1913, New York, New York, No. 4.

DISSERTATIONS

Osborne, Peter, *Russel Farnum Lord: His Life, His Times, His Letters.* senior honors project, unpublished manuscript, Rutgers - The State University, Newark, New Jersey, 1982.

NEWSPAPER ARTICLES

Fort Decker: Landmark Named Historic Site, Newburgh Evening News, Newburgh, New York, December 26, 1974.

179 Years Young, Fort Decker Waits To Return To 1793, Port Jervis

Union Gazette, Port Jervis, New York, June 2, 1972.

Tablet on Old Stone House: Impressive Unveiling Ceremonies at Germantown,, Port Jervis Union, Port Jervis, New York.May 16, 1908.

Tablet on Old Stone House, Port Jervis Union, Port Jervis, New York, May 16, 1908.

Negro Slave Defended Mistress in Stone Fort, Middletown Daily Time-Press, October 17, 1925.

The Old Stone House: Germantown's Historic Building, The Port Jervis Union, Port Jervis, New York, May 26, 1893.

Forts Once Dotted Tri-State Region, Calvin Van Etten Crane Collection and Files, undated newspaper article with no source given.

A Bit Of Local History: Brief Sketch of the Old Stone House in Germantown, Port Jervis Evening Gazette, Port Jervis, New York, August 13, 1887.

A Relic of Pioneer Days: A Romance of the Old Stone House in Germantown, The Port Jervis Gazette, Port Jervis, New York, February 16, 1903.

Decker Fort, or Stone House, Built in 1793, Saved by Firemen, The Port Jervis Gazette, Port Jervis, New York, January 22, 1924.

Historical Society Accepts Keys to Fort, Union Gazette, Port Jervis, New York, May 27, 1970.

Nails 110 Years Old, Port Jervis Union, Port Jervis, New York, June 24, 1903.

Old Stone House Revisited, Port Jervis Union Gazette, Port Jervis, New York,October 2, 1972,

Port Asked to Consider Museum at Decker's Fort, Port Jervis Union Gazette, Port Jervis, New York, December 10, 1966.

Port's Oldest Building On National Register,   Port Jervis Union Gazette, Port Jervis, New York, July 23, 1974.
What's Buried in the Basement of Fort Decker, TheGazette, Port Jervis, New York October 27, 1995.

INTERVIEWS

Auerbach, Mrs. Chana c. 1990
Collette, Flojean. Interviews by author, 1990-2004.
Coslick, Bud. Interview by author, 1980s.
Fleming, Leo, City of Port Jervis Fire Inspector, Interview by author, September 1, 1988.
Hammond, Doris. Interview by author, 1990s.
Hornbeck, Jacob. Interviews by author, 1980s.
Kranz, Betty. Interviews by author. 1980s.

LETTERS

Bello, Nancy to Alan White, July 2, 2001, FDMOHC.
Carey, C. Richard to Peter Osborne, Notes on Martinus Decker in the 1798 Federal Assessment for the Town of Minisink, undated, FDMOHC
Mallalieu, John to Peter Osborne, July 20, 2005. FDMOHC.
Vail, Roy to Cornelius Cuddeback, President, Minisink Valley Historical Society, undated, FDMOC.
Carpentier, Donald to Richard Tarbell, Vice President, Minisink Valley Historical Society, January 16, 1980, FDMOHC.

ARCHIVES

Collection of the Minisink Valley Historical Society, 138 Pike Street and The Fort Decker Museum of History Collection,127

West Main Street, Port Jervis, New York.

George Washington Papers, Series 4, Reel 56, February 10, 1779-March 25, 1779, Library of Congress, Washington, D.C.

National Archives and Records Administration, Washington, D.C.

Orange County Government Center, Route 207, Hall of Records, Goshen, New York

INTERNET

Haynes Archives, Compiled by Kenneth Bigolin, RootsWeb.com, April 29, 2005.

Passenger and Immigration Lists Index, 1500-1900s, Ancestry.com, February 14, 2005.

MISCELLANEOUS

Coroner's Report 1916, Orange County Supervisor's Report, 1917, Goshen, New York.

Obituary, Mary Cannon, Port Jervis Union, Port Jervis, New York, March 10, 1916.

Obituary, John Cannon, Port Jervis Union, Port Jervis, New York, March 19, 1915.

Accidental Shooting: Stanley Canfield Wounded In Neck By A Boy Companion, Port Jervis Union, Port Jervis New York, August 17, 1903.

Deaths and Funerals: Mrs. Sarah M. Campfield, Port Jervis Union Gazette, Port Jervis, New York, December 16, 1956.

Deaths and Funerals: C. Mose Campfield, Port Jervis Union Gazette, Port Jervis, New York. June 1, 1971.

Obituary: Mrs. Moses Campfield, Port Jervis Union Gazette, Port

Jervis, New York.February 7, 1975.

Death of Mrs. Stephen St. John, The Family Gazette, Port Jervis, New York, April 26, 1870.

Hayne Family History, William J. Coulter's Wantage Recorder Collection, Collection of the Minisink Valley Historical Society, 138 Pike Street, Port Jervis, New York.

Little Stanley Campfield Succumbs to His Injuries, Port Jervis Union, Port Jervis, New York, September 29, 1903.

Wilhelmus Westfall Genealogy, William Coulter, Photocopy, *Captain Wilhelmus Westfall 1753-1796: His Genealogical History* by Dudley Ham, 37 Winterest Way, N. Ft. Myers, Florida, April 10, 1995.

James McCoy's Abstract of Sussex County Deeds, East Jersey Deeds, Amboy S-4, Sussex County Hall of Records, Newton, New Jersey.

Report on the Proposed Use of an Abandoned Burial Ground for the Erection of A School House at Port Jervis, New York State Board of Health, Extracted from Fifth Annual Report, 1884.

Obituary, Stephen St. John, Family Gazette, Port Jervis, New York, unpaginated. September 8, 1870.

Stephen St. John Family Genealogy and Burial Locations, compiled by Nancy Conod, January 15, 2006.

Stickney, Charles. *A Minisink Double Wedding,* Wantage Record, undated manuscript, MVHS.

The Old Stone House in Germantown, Clark, Lewis and Edward Ruttenber, **History of Orange County, New York.** Philadelphia: Everts & Peck, 1881.

Descendants of Jan Gerritson Decker and his wife Grietje Hendricks Westercamp by Mrs. Harvey Cole, MVHS.

Genealogical Exchange, Caskey Family Listing, The New York Genealogical and Biographical Record, Vol 106, No. 3, July 1975, New York, New York.

Martinus Decker Pension Application, Revolutionary War Pension Record R.7158, New York, National Archives and Records Administration, Washington, D.C.

Martin Cuykendall Pension Application, Revolutionary War Pension Record S-12649, New York, National Archives and Records Administration, North Carolina State Library (Raleigh), Series M804, Roll #727.

Benjamin Davis Pension Application, Revolutionary War Pension Record S-23187, New York, National Archives and Records Administration, North Carolina State Library (Raleigh), Series M804, Roll #750.

Wilhelmus Westfall Pension Application, Revolutionary War Pension Record S-15322, New York, North Carolina State Library (Raleigh) Series M-804, Roll # 2538

Gabriel DiGiantamasco to Minisink Valley Historical Society, Liber 2212 p. 300, Orange County Government Center, Goshen, New York.

Betty Kranz to Minisink Valley Historical Society, Liber 2809 p. 274, Orange County Government Center, Goshen, New York.

William and Linda McCann to the Minisink Valley Historical Society, Liber 2176, p. 913, Orange County Government Center, Goshen, New York.

Martinus and Mary Decker to Martinus Decker Jr., Deed dated September 15, 1798, FDMOHC

Richard Decker to John Kent, Deed numbered R-77-1815, Orange County Government Center, Goshen, New York.

John Kent to Stephen St. John and Benjamin Dodge, Deed numbered U-37-1819, Orange County Government Center, Goshen, New York.

Executors of the Estate of Stephen St. John to John Cannon, Sr, Deed numbered 243-395-1872, Orange County Government Center, Goshen, New York.

Gertrude L. Kellam, administratrix of the Estate of Lauretta Lyons, James Lyons and Raymond Lyons to the Minisink Valley Historical Society, Liber 1846, p. 487, Orange County Government Center, Goshen, New York.

Handwritten notes by Cornelius Cuddeback, a former president of the Society, undated.

ACKNOWLEDGMENTS

This book is the result of the efforts of a number of people and organizations. First and foremost, I am grateful to my wife Janis who has always served as my editor and allowed me to slip on some of my chores when I am working on research projects. I am also grateful to the readers of the manuscript: my wife, Janis, Nancy Conod, Nancy Vocci, Charles Swartwout, Mark Hendrickson, Robert Aber, Flojean Collette, and Barbara and Fred Johnson Weissman. Nancy C and Nancy V also helped to conduct extensive research into the various family genealogies that are outlined here, along with researching the various properties that now make up the Fort Decker compound. Both offered their unvarnished opinions if they felt I had not clearly elucidated an idea.

Rick Hibberd assisted greatly with the layout of the book, designed the cover, and helped make this a much better book graphically. He also offered his candid advice during the course of the project, which was gratefully accepted. New York Senator John Bonacic secured funding for the programs undertaken by Upper Delaware Scenic Byway, and this allowed for the printing of the book. We are grateful to both Senator Bonacic, a friend to our Society, and the Upper Delaware Scenic Byway for their support.

The author is grateful to the Port Jervis Area Heritage Commission for allowing the author to extensively quote from the 1993 publication that I wrote for them entitled *The Port Jervis Area Heritage Commission Salutes the Decker Stone House 1793-1993.* The Minisink Valley Historical Society provided for the use of its large collection of photographs and historical materials. My thanks to the board of directors for allowing me to spend the time that was necessary to bring this book to fruition.

The author wants to acknowledge the important and vital research done by Romayne B. Perritte, a member of our Society, who transcribed the volumes of material that make up Martinus Decker's Revolutionary War pension application and depositions. She graciously shared all of her files on Martinus Decker which proved to be very helpful. I also want to remember a very promising intern that our Society had - Jess Novak - who also transcribed a large amount of hand-written records that have found their way into the volume on Martinus Decker's service records. Mark Hendrickson found a number of pension records describing Fort Decker at the time of the Revolution. His discoveries are among the most significant in this book. He also helped digitally prepare pension records for inclusion in this book and has contributed greatly to our knowledge of the Battle at Minisink through other research.

The following individuals provided research materials or helped in researching various archives to obtain materials used in this book over the last twenty-seven years: Cornelius

Cuddeback, Gertrude Kellam, Roger King, Charles King, Raymond Lyons, Richard Tarbell, Allan Berner, Thomas Leek, Clarence Edwards, Miral Haubner, Robert Longcore, Kevin Stroyan, John Mallalieu, Wayne Caskey, Grace Lee Roosa, Robert Edwards, Mead and Mary Stapler, the Office of the Orange County Historian, Theodore Sly, C. Richard Carey, the Neversink Valley Area Museum, Richard Roberts, Donald Mavros, Charles Swartwout, John and Susan Trumbull, members of the Old Mine Road Chapter, National Society Daughters of the American Revolution, Ray Decker, Ethel and Jacob Hornbeck, George Greiner, George Fluhr, Linda Zimmermann, Michael Worden, Walpack Historical Society, Lance Grach, the Navasink Longrifles, Kelly Millspaugh, Joanna Szakmary, Fort Delaware, Zak Szakmary, Betty Kranz, Adista Theodore, Don Parker, Gray-Parker Funeral Home, Richard Quick, Dr. Frank Simpson, William Bavoso, Ray Close, Frank Salvati, Dudley Ham, Florence Gray, Brian Lewis, William Clark, Gordon Hobbs, Ray Decker, Walpack Historical Society, William Doyle, Nicole Novak, Doris Hammond, William Hunt, Robert Hockenberry, Caroline Baumel, Shirley Shay Basham, Mim and Jim Carpenter and Robert Aber. We also acknowledge the excellent work done by the volunteers of the Orange County Chapter of the New York State Archaeological Association because their work opened new avenues of discussion about the building's history. Flojean Campfield Collette provided a great deal of family materials to the author that helped to enhance the story of the stone house in the 20th century.

The author also would like to note the efforts of many area residents who over the years have visited our site, and provided significant amounts of material incorporated into this booklet; they have helped preserve the building and participate in programs on the site. To all of these people, we offer our sincere thanks for making this book possible.

ABOUT THE AUTHOR

Peter Osborne has been the executive director of the Minisink Valley Historical Society for more than twenty-six years. He has written frequently about items of a local and regional historical nature. His interest in Fort Decker comes from his love of old buildings, and from having spent many hours working in it and around the grounds. He has a Bachelor of Arts degree from Rutgers, the State University of New Jersey, with a special interest in the Great Depression era and the Roosevelts - Theodore, Franklin and Eleanor.

Most recently he has written about the Civilian Conservation Corps, a New Deal agency created by President Franklin Delano Roosevelt to fight the effects of the depression. He is married to Janis Osborne, the retired editor of the weekly newspaper, *TheGazette* and author of **Put The Dog On The Phone: The Collected Newspaper Columns of Janis Osborne**. He has a son, Ryan, by a previous marriage, and three stepchildren, Megan, Tom and Mike and fifteen step-grandchildren.

The Society continues to seek information about the history of its stone house museum. If you have additional material about the building or the families that lived in it please feel free to contact the author and the Society at:

Minisink Valley Historical Society
Post Office Box 659
127-131 West Main Street
Port Jervis, New York 12771
Phone: 845-856-2375
Email Address: history@minisink.org

Courtesy Shirley Shay Basham

The Shay Milk Wagon sits in front of Fort Decker at the turn of the century.